Editor
Erica N. Russikoff, M.A.

Editor in Chief
Ina Massler Levin, M.A.

Creative Director
Karen J. Goldfluss, M.S. Ed.

Illustrator
Clint McKnight

Cover Artist
Brenda DiAntonis

Art Coordinator
Renée Mc Elwee

Imaging
James Edward Grace
Craig Gunnell

Publisher
Mary D. Smith, M.S. Ed.

MATH STO
to use with your
English Language Learners

TCR 2908

F-2

Contains Standards and Benchmarks

- Provides sample activities and lessons
- Tailored to help ELLs as well as native English speakers
- Includes ELL strategies and skills for teachers and students

Teacher Created Resources

Author
Tracie I. Heskett, M. Ed.

Teacher Created Resources
6421 Industry Way
Westminster, CA 92683
www.teachercreated.com
ISBN: 978-1-4206-2908-8

© 2012 Teacher Created Resources
Made in U.S.A.

Teacher Created Resources

Table of Contents

Table of Contents *(cont.)*

Introduction

Teachers across the country are experiencing increasing numbers of English language learners (ELLs) in their regular education classrooms. As ELL student populations grow, teachers need strategies to reach these students. Many lessons in existing curricula are designed for native speakers of English and are not tailored to support second language acquisition. The lessons and strategies in this book accommodate the needs of ELLs.

Math Strategies to Use With Your English Language Learners offers teachers ways to teach specific math concepts and skills to ELLs and at-risk students in regular education classrooms. This book includes math teaching strategies and skills, two glossaries of common math terms and verbs, and sample lessons and activities. The purpose of this book is to help teachers make math lessons comprehensible to their ELL students.

The following are a few of the most frequently asked questions regarding ELL math instruction. The answers provided are general; for more specific answers, review the strategies in this book.

How do specific strategies help ELL students develop math skills?

Instructional strategies that focus on math and language skills support ELLs as they build English proficiency. Support in students' first language skills helps students develop their understanding of math concepts in English. Effective teaching strategies engage students and increase their motivation to learn.

Why is it that some ELLs are able to give answers to questions, but they can't explain how they arrived at the conclusions?

Various cultures approach math processes in different ways. The focus may be on arriving at the correct answer, rather than the steps students take to find the answer. In these cases, teachers will need to teach students how to explain their thought processes and answers.

How can I use interactive whiteboard technology to help my ELLs?

Interactive whiteboard technology can be an invaluable resource when working with ELLs. ELL instruction is often visually oriented; pictures, graphics, and other visual information help to increase student comprehension. Use interactive whiteboard technology to enhance the following:

- ✪ add variety to visual aids and graphic organizers.
- ✪ provide sentence frames for different language levels.
- ✪ help students mark text.
- ✪ display charts and tables.
- ✪ help students make connections between written and oral text.

How to Use This Book

The first section, *English Language Learner Instruction*, contains information on recognizing learning styles and establishing cultural connections. It also includes specific math skills that your students can learn and use independently. Tips for how to use instructional tools, such as manipulatives and technology, are also provided in this section. Additionally, this section addresses specific strategies teachers can use with their ELLs. A few of the strategies detailed are Mnemonic Strategies, Numbered Heads, and Sentence Frames. Each strategy page includes an explanation, examples, tips for teaching, and at least one sample activity.

The second section, *Math Language Connections*, contains vocabulary tips and activities, acknowledging that students need to understand math vocabulary in order to succeed in math. Also included are two glossaries—one of math terms and the other of math verbs. These glossaries are student-friendly, in that they contain definitions written in a simplified way (some definitions even have accompanying pictures). While you can use these glossaries as your own instructional tool, you may also wish to copy them for your students so they have a math resource to consult. A chart on confusing language patterns will help teachers understand some of the language obstacles ELLs face, as well as how to help students overcome them. This section concludes with a thorough review of how to help students "crack the code" of word problems.

The third section, *Practical Classroom Applications*, is composed of sample lessons and information on assessment. Lessons include vocabulary and materials lists, as well as activity directions, handouts, and extensions. The resources, activities, and lessons provided will help you to incorporate ELL teaching strategies into math lessons.

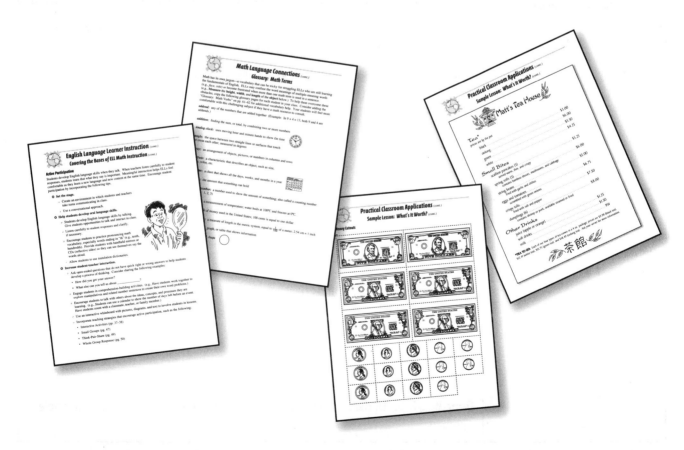

Standards and Benchmarks

Each activity in *Math Strategies to Use With Your English Language Learners* meets at least one of the following standards and benchmarks, which are used with permission from McREL. Copyright 2012 McREL. Mid-continent Research for Education and Learning, 4601 DTC Boulevard, Suite 500, Denver, Colorado 80237. Telephone: 303-337-0990. Website: *www.mcrel.org/standards-benchmarks*. To align McREL Standards to the Common Core Standards, go to *www.mcrel.org*.

Standards	Benchmarks
Standard 1. Uses a variety of strategies in the problem-solving process	**Benchmark 1.** Draws pictures to represent problems **Benchmark 2.** Uses discussions with teachers and other students to understand problems **Benchmark 3.** Explains to others how she or he went about solving a numerical problem **Benchmark 4.** Makes organized lists or tables of information necessary for solving a problem **Benchmark 5.** Uses whole number models (e.g., pattern blocks, tiles, or other manipulative materials) to represent problems
Standard 2. Understands and applies basic and advanced properties of the concepts of numbers	**Benchmark 1.** Understands that numerals are symbols used to represent quantities or attributes of real-world objects **Benchmark 2.** Counts whole numbers (i.e., both cardinal and ordinal numbers) **Benchmark 3.** Understands symbolic, concrete, and pictorial representations of numbers (e.g., written numerals, objects in sets, number lines) **Benchmark 4.** Uses base-ten concepts to compare whole number relationships (e.g., 4 is less than 10, 30 is 3 tens) and represent them in flexible ways (e.g., expanded form, decomposing numbers) **Benchmark 5.** Understands the concept of a unit and its subdivision into equal parts (e.g., one object, such as a candy bar, and its division into equal parts to be shared among four people)
Standard 3. Uses basic and advanced procedures while performing the processes of computation	**Benchmark 1.** Adds and subtracts whole numbers **Benchmark 2.** Solves real-world problems involving addition and subtraction of whole numbers **Benchmark 3.** Understands basic estimation strategies (e.g., using reference sets, using front-end digits) and terms (e.g., "about," "near," "closer to," "between," "a little less than") **Benchmark 4.** Understands the inverse relationship between addition and subtraction **Benchmark 5.** Understands strategies for the addition and subtraction of whole numbers

Standards and Benchmarks *(cont.)*

Standards	Benchmarks
Standard 4. Understands and applies basic and advanced properties of the concepts of measurement	**Benchmark 1.** Understands the basic measures length, width, height, weight, and temperature **Benchmark 2.** Understands the concept of time and how it is measured **Benchmark 3.** Knows processes for telling time, counting money, and measuring length, weight, and temperature, using basic standard and non-standard units **Benchmark 4.** Makes quantitative estimates of familiar linear dimensions, weights, and time intervals and checks them against measurements
Standard 5. Understands and applies basic and advanced properties of the concepts of geometry	**Benchmark 1.** Understands basic properties of simple geometric shapes (e.g., number of sides, corners, square corners) and similarities and differences between simple geometric shapes **Benchmark 2.** Understands the common language of spatial sense (e.g., "left," "right," "horizontal," "in front of") **Benchmark 3.** Uses the names of simple geometric shapes (e.g., circles, squares, triangles) to represent and describe real world situations **Benchmark 4.** Understands that patterns can be made by putting different shapes together or taking them apart
Standard 6. Understands and applies basic and advanced concepts of statistics and data analysis	**Benchmark 1.** Collects and represents information about objects or events in simple graphs **Benchmark 2.** Understands that one can find out about a group of things by studying just a few of them
Standard 7. Understands and applies basic and advanced concepts of probability	**Benchmark 1.** Understands that some events are more likely to happen than others **Benchmark 2.** Understands that some events can be predicted fairly well but others cannot because we do not always know everything that may affect an event
Standard 8. Understands and applies basic and advanced properties of functions and algebra	**Benchmark 1.** Recognizes regularities in a variety of contexts (e.g., events, designs, shapes, sets of numbers) **Benchmark 2.** Extends simple patterns (e.g., of numbers, physical objects, geometric shapes)

ESL Terms

The following are some of the most common terms used in ESL instruction. These terms are used throughout this book. For definitions of specific skills or strategies (e.g., classifying, math journals, think-pair-share), look on pp. 21–27 and 34–50.

Academic language: language used in the school environment, including words, phrases, grammar, and language structure, as well as academic terms and technical language

BICS: Basic Interpersonal Communication Skills; social, conversational language used with family and friends

Bilingual: speaking two languages fluently

CALP: Cognitive Academic Language Proficiency; formal language used in classrooms and with texts

Chunks/Chunking: information divided into units in order to be more comprehensible

Decoding: skills used (such as transfer) to decipher given information into understandable information

Differentiated instruction: modified instruction so that students of different abilities, knowledge, and skills can equally experience materials (e.g., providing multiple assignments within a teaching unit that are tailored for students with differing language levels)

EFL: English as a Foreign Language

ELL: English Language Learner

ESL: English as a Second Language

Explicit instruction: otherwise known as "direct instruction"; learners are provided with specific information or directions about what is to be learned.

Fluency: ability to read, write, and speak a language easily, naturally, and accurately

Language acquisition: the natural process of learning a language; second language acquisition usually includes formal study

Language proficiency: ability to communicate and understand oral (listening and speaking) and written (reading and writing) academic and nonacademic language

Multicultural: relating to multiple cultural groups

Native language: first language learned and spoken

Native speakers of English (or native English speakers): individuals whose first language is English

Realia: real objects used for tactile demonstrations and for improving students' understanding (e.g., bringing in household examples of three-dimensional items in the shapes of cubes, pyramids, spheres, etc.)

Transfer (as in language transfer): applying knowledge and skills from a first language to a second language

Wait time: amount of time that elapses between a question or instruction and the next verbal response

ESL Objectives

Standards-based instruction aligns lessons with standards that state what students should know and be able to do. In addition to these standards that apply to all students, it is helpful to identify specific objectives for your English language learners. Incorporating goals, such as those listed here, will enable you to include ELLs in lessons and learning activities and ensure they are developing skills that will help them be successful.

- ✪ Students use English verbal and nonverbal communication to express ideas, give and receive information, and participate in classroom activities.

- ✪ Students listen, imitate, question, and seek support and feedback from others as they learn to listen, speak, read, and write in English.

- ✪ Students practice their English language skills by using context to make meaning.

- ✪ Students learn to use English to follow oral and written directions, ask questions, participate in class discussions, and interact with others to accomplish classroom tasks.

- ✪ Students use English to gather information through listening, speaking, reading, and writing.

- ✪ Students use English to demonstrate knowledge orally and in writing and to respond to the learning of others.

- ✪ Students use learning strategies and skills across the language domains to understand and apply English skills to academic subject matter.

- ✪ Students observe, model, experiment with, and seek feedback about how to speak and behave in the classroom setting.

Q & A: Instructional Goals

The following Q & A addresses a few of the most frequently asked questions regarding instructional goals for ELLs.

What are the instructional goals for English language learners in math?

- ✪ Participate in math experiences.

- ✪ Develop academic language skills in this content area.

- ✪ Develop an understanding of math concepts.

- ✪ Comprehend math vocabulary.

- ✪ Apply vocabulary and skills to solve problems.

- ✪ Use the language of mathematics to communicate their learning orally and in writing.

How can I help my students meet math standards and instructional goals?

- ✪ Conduct a needs assessment at the beginning of the year or unit to determine students' familiarity with concepts.

- ✪ Post goals and objectives on the board to help ELLs keep track of and monitor their progress.

- ✪ Simplify language and incorporate visuals as needed to help students understand concepts.

- ✪ Determine the language skills that students will need for each lesson prior to teaching the lesson.

- ✪ Incorporate ESL objectives (pg. 9) into math lessons.

- ✪ Include how students will use math vocabulary as part of language goals. (e.g., Students will express orally or in writing why they chose a particular strategy to solve a problem.)

- ✪ Differentiate instruction. Provide appropriate activities for each child to learn, based on his or her needs.

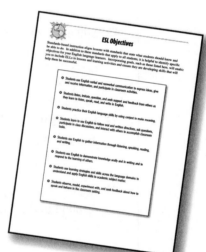

Q & A: Instructional Goals (cont.)

Which teaching strategies can I use to meet specific learning goals?

Learning Goal	Strategy
Participate in math experiences	Asking Questions (pg. 34) Interactive Activities (pp. 37–38) Numbered Heads (pg. 44) Small Groups (pg. 47) Think-Alouds (pg. 48) Whole-Group Response (pg. 50)
Develop academic language skills	Graphic Organizers (pg. 36) Mnemonic Strategies (pg. 42) Sentence Frames (pg. 46) Small Groups (pg. 47)
Develop understanding of math concepts	Brainstorming (pg. 35) Models (pg. 42) Peer Tutoring (pg. 45) Think-Pair-Share (pg. 49) Visual Aids (pg. 50) Whole-Group Response (pg. 50)
Comprehend math vocabulary	Graphic Organizers (pg. 36) Interactive Activities (pp. 37–38) Marking Text (pp. 39–40) Visual Aids (pg. 50)
Apply vocabulary and skills to solve problems	Asking Questions (pg. 34) Brainstorming (pg. 35) Interactive Activities (pp. 37–38) Multisensory Activities (pg. 43) Peer Tutoring (pg. 45) Small Groups (pg. 47) Think-Pair-Share (pg. 49) Visual Aids (pg. 50)
Express learning orally and in writing	Graphic Organizers (pg. 36) Math Journals (pg. 41) Numbered Heads (pg. 44) Sentence Frames (pg. 46) Small Groups (pg. 47) Think-Pair-Share (pg. 49) Whole-Group Response (pg. 50)

The Four Language Domains

TESOL's (Teachers of English to Speakers of Other Languages) language proficiency standards are divided into four language domains: listening, speaking, reading, and writing. They are listed in the order in which students become proficient. Below each language domain are activities targeted to support language development.

Listening

- ✪ Have students listen to other students explain their thinking in math.
- ✪ Have students hear more than one voice in English to develop strong listening skills.
- ✪ Have students follow along with print copies when problems are read aloud in class. Students can underline words or phrases they don't understand for clarification.

Speaking

- ✪ Speak more slowly and pause often.
- ✪ Paraphrase, if necessary.
- ✪ Have students express their thinking one-on-one or in small groups rather than in front of the whole class.
- ✪ Ask volunteers to talk through a mental math process to practice speaking.
- ✪ Have students explain their thinking aloud rather than the teacher paraphrasing for them.

Reading

- ✪ Ask students to read directions or problems aloud for the class. Pair up students, if necessary.
- ✪ Simplify word problems.
- ✪ Help students read the board or class charts by writing numbers legibly.
- ✪ Provide opportunities for students to read math-related materials.

Writing

- ✪ Teach students to write numbers clearly.
- ✪ Have students write as they explain or share their responses with the class (instead of the teacher writing as the student talks).
- ✪ Give students opportunities to write about math.
- ✪ Have students write descriptions using math vocabulary.
- ✪ Model how to write word problems and explanations for solutions.

English Language Learner Instruction
Covering the Bases of ELL Math Instruction

Background knowledge, comprehensible instruction, and active participation are the "bases," or main components, of effective ELL math instruction. Accomplishing all three results in a "home run" of understanding for your students. Incorporate the suggestions and examples on the following pages when planning lessons to address the three major components of ELL instruction, specifically as they apply to math class.

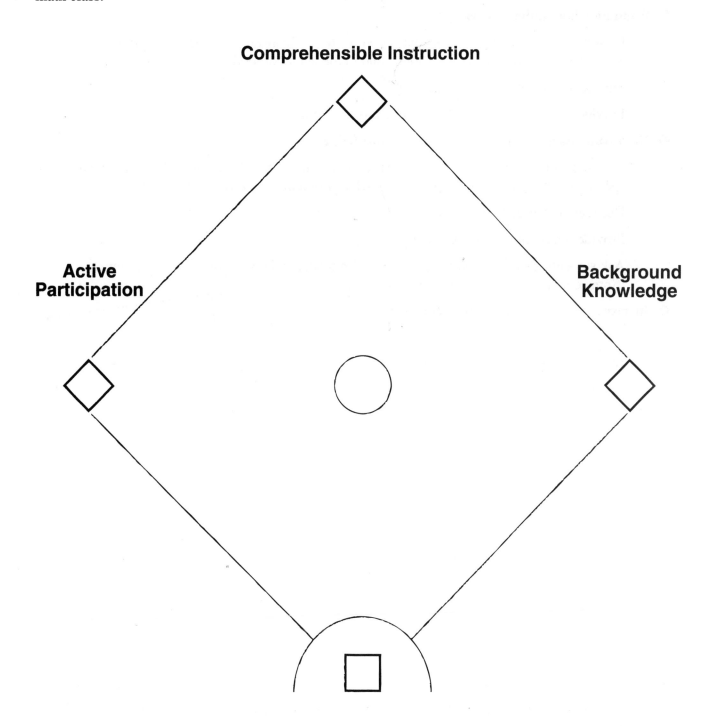

English Language Learner Instruction *(cont.)*
Covering the Bases of ELL Math Instruction *(cont.)*

Background Knowledge

What students already know about a topic affects how well they learn new concepts. Help ELLs access their background knowledge and make connections to relevant math topics by incorporating the following tips.

- ✪ **Build on what students already know.**

  - ★ Prior knowledge helps students connect with a text. Be aware of students' previous experiences in the classroom, at home, and in the neighborhood.

  - ★ Start with students' previous learning.

  - ★ Provide relevant background knowledge for the context.

- ✪ **Help students access their background knowledge.**

  - ★ Use student questions to build background knowledge. (e.g., Create a K-W-L chart on a specific math topic or vocabulary term, such as *estimate*, *place value*, or *weight*.)

  - ★ Use real objects and visual aids.

  - ★ Provide opportunities to talk about math.

  - ★ Ask students about their past experiences with math and how to solve math problems. (Some countries do not teach "show your work.")

- ✪ **Increase students' background knowledge.**

  - ★ Use contextual clues.

  - ★ Build background between vocabulary and text.

  - ★ Build background knowledge with first-hand experiences. Have students share their experiences with a topic. (e.g., Have students describe their experiences with geometric shapes in their cultures and home lives. Students may already be familiar with many shapes and how they work, without having the precise vocabulary needed for learning geometry in the classroom.)

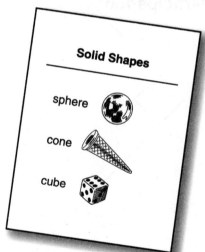

Solid Shapes

sphere

cone

cube

English Language Learner Instruction *(cont.)*
Covering the Bases of ELL Math Instruction *(cont.)*

Comprehensible Instruction

Instruction is comprehensible to students when they understand most of what the teacher says. Incorporate background knowledge, present new information in context, and use visual aids to increase students' comprehension. Help students understand lesson content and activities by incorporating the following tips.

- ✪ **Provide instruction students can understand.**
  - ★ Make sure students have the language background needed to understand the lesson.
  - ★ Reword text as needed to make it easier for students to read.
  - ★ Explain a concept more than once using different words, explanations, and examples.
  - ★ Teach the specific vocabulary needed for the lesson.
    - Clearly label and point to each part of a tally, pictograph, or simple bar graph to teach students specific vocabulary words. Use charts or graphs that students have created in class with their own data and some vocabulary students already know, such as favorite colors or months in which students have birthdays.

- ✪ **Provide appropriate context for instruction.**
  - ★ Present new concepts in context.
  - ★ Listen carefully to students and present information in a context that draws on students' personal experiences.
  - ★ Incorporate visual aids (pg. 50).

- ✪ **Give meaningful feedback.**
  - ★ Ask students to repeat back for clarification.
  - ★ Redirect students' questions back to the class.
  - ★ Provide opportunities for verbal interaction in the classroom.
  - ★ Allow students to express their ideas.
  - ★ Ask students to share how they solved specific math problems.
  - ★ Phrase feedback in such a way that students can understand.

Active Participation

Students develop English language skills when they talk. When teachers listen carefully to student responses, students learn that what they say is important. Meaningful interaction helps ELLs feel comfortable as they learn a new language and new content at the same time. Encourage student participation by incorporating the following tips.

✪ **Set the stage.**

   ★ Create an environment in which students and teachers take turns communicating in class.

   ★ Use a conversational approach.

✪ **Help students develop oral language skills.**

   ★ Students develop English language skills by talking. Give students opportunities to talk and interact in class.

   ★ Listen carefully to student responses and clarify, if necessary.

   ★ Encourage students to practice pronouncing math vocabulary, especially words ending in "th" (e.g., tenth, hundredth). Provide students with handheld mirrors or CDs (reflective sides) so they can see themselves say the words aloud.

   ★ Allow students to use translation dictionaries.

✪ **Increase student-teacher interaction.**

   ★ Ask open-ended questions that do not have quick right or wrong answers to help students develop a process of thinking. Consider sharing the following examples:

   • How did you get your answer?

   • What else can you tell us about _____?

   ★ Engage students in comprehension-building activities. (e.g., Have students work together to explore manipulatives and related number sentences to create their own word problems.)

   ★ Encourage students to talk with others about the ideas, concepts, and processes they are learning. (e.g., Students can use a calendar to show the number of days left before an event. Have students count with a classmate, teacher, or family member.)

   ★ Use an interactive whiteboard with pictures, diagrams, and text to involve students in lessons.

   ★ Incorporate teaching strategies that encourage active participation, such as the following:

   • Interactive Activities (pp. 37–38)

   • Small Groups (pg. 47)

   • Think-Pair-Share (pg. 49)

   • Whole-Group Response (pg. 50)

English Language Learner Instruction *(cont.)*
Recognizing Learning Styles

Students have many different learning styles, or ways in which they acquire information most effectively. Use the "Learning Styles Inventory" on pg. 18 to have students think about how they learn. Student answers can be used to guide lesson planning. Implement a variety of teaching methods, such as those suggested in the chart below, to expose students to many different learning and teaching styles. A diverse learning experience gives ELLs support while learning a new language. Have students work individually, with partners, in small groups, and as a class. Consider environmental factors, such as light, noise, distractions, and amount of workspace to meet student needs and learning preferences.

Teach to the Type

Visual	Auditory
Students learn and remember what they see. • Use body language and facial expressions to communicate meaning. • Use charts, diagrams, graphics, pictures, video clips from the Internet or DVDs, and examples to provide students with visual examples of concepts. • Draw sketches when setting up math problems to give students a visual aid. • Use color to distinguish between different concepts in an explanation. • Incorporate drawing or simple art projects in math class. • Use colored pencils or crayons when teaching two-digit addition or subtraction. (Write the tens and ones in different colors.)	**Students learn and remember what they hear.** • Use tone of voice and rate of speech to communicate meaning. • Provide oral explanations. • Read textbook passages out loud. • Have students participate in class discussions. • Allow students to work in small groups. • Help auditory learners focus by removing other auditory distractions. • Use songs or chants to teach rote concepts or to review math facts. • Have students practice skip-counting using jump ropes. • Have students talk out loud when solving math problems so they can hear their thinking processes.

Kinesthetic / Tactile
Students learn and remember through touching, feeling, and movement. • Use manipulative materials (pp. 28–29).   • Incorporate movement to teach concepts.   • Use gestures in class.   • Have students physically move and arrange themselves to demonstrate ordinal numbers.   • Have students measure different materials, such as cornmeal, oats, flour, dry beans, water, or sand to explore measurement.

English Language Learner Instruction (cont.)
Recognizing Learning Styles (cont.)

Learning Styles Inventory

How do I determine students' learning styles?

- ✪ Listen to the descriptive words students use in casual conversation.
- ✪ Observe classroom behavior.
- ✪ Conduct a simple learning styles inventory.

To help identify your students' learning styles, photocopy this page, cutting off the top section and enlarging as necessary. Tell students you want them to think about what works best for them when they solve math problems. Write one or two sample challenging math problems on the board if helpful for your students.

Read each statement aloud to the students and have them respond by placing check marks or drawing smiling faces next to each statement that is true for them. Use the completed inventories to assess your students' learning styles individually and as a group.

✂ -

Directions: Listen to each statement as it is read to you. Draw a smiling face or put a check mark next to each statement that is **true** for you.

_____ It is easier for me to understand a math problem if I write it out or draw a picture.

_____ It is easier to understand a math problem when I hear the teacher repeat the problem out loud.

_____ I can understand math problems if I move objects around to show what is happening in the problem.

_____ When I learn something new in math, it helps me if I see a picture, chart, or other diagram.

_____ It is easier to learn something new in math if I can talk about it with someone else.

_____ When I learn something new in math, I like to watch someone else work through the problem and then try it myself.

_____ I wish the teacher would write out the problems so we could read them.

_____ I wish the teacher would read aloud the problems before we start to work.

_____ I would like it if the teacher would show us more demonstrations with objects.

_____ Please let me use drawings so I can know how to do the problem.

_____ Please let us use objects to figure out problems.

English Language Learner Instruction *(cont.)*
Engaging Students in Learning

Children learn more when they are actively engaged in their learning. Student engagement occurs at the following three levels:

- ✪ *behavioral*—the effort students put forth to participate

- ✪ *emotional*—how well students feel they belong in the classroom

- ✪ *cognitive*—how much students invest in their own learning

Provide opportunities for students to observe, listen, speak, think, read, write, draw, and experiment with new concepts. Motivate students with the following engaging learning environments:

Before
Build background knowledge.
Communicate high expectations to students.
Establish expectations for active involvement. (e.g., Have students participate in physical activities, such as writing, moving, or acting out to express their understanding of lesson objectives.)
Make sure students understand that it's good to take risks and try new problem-solving methods.

During
Monitor student engagement and adjust lessons accordingly.
Physically place students in the room so they are more focused and interested in lessons.
Ask questions (pg. 34).
Use small group interactions (pg. 47) to give students a safe environment in which to practice and use math vocabulary.
Use interactive teaching strategies, such as think-pair-share (pg. 49), whole-group response (pg. 50), small groups (pg. 47), and manipulatives (pp. 28–29).
Incorporate multimedia and technology into lessons (pg. 33).

After
Have students repeat explanations to the teacher.
Invite students to talk about shared learning experiences.

Apply New Learning
Incorporate thematic instruction to help students relate math concepts to other learning throughout the day.
Provide opportunities for students to express their new learning, specifically math terms and concepts.
Encourage students to explore how they can apply math to their everyday lives.
Challenge students to identify ways they can use what they learn in math to help others.

English Language Learner Instruction *(cont.)*
Establishing Cultural Connections

Math presents two challenges to ELL students: learning new math concepts and learning a new language. For this reason, it's important for teachers to acknowledge and accommodate English language learners' native languages and cultures.

Recognize native languages and support translation, as needed.

- ✪ Read directions or provide written directions in students' native languages.

- ✪ Provide bilingual dictionaries or picture glossaries to help students learn new vocabulary.

- ✪ Allow students to clarify new concepts in their native languages, if possible.

- ✪ Allow students to complete some work in their native languages, if possible.

- ✪ Encourage students to offer each other bilingual support.

- ✪ Encourage students to discuss their homework with family members using their native languages.

Acknowledge and incorporate students' cultures and backgrounds.

- ✪ Relate concepts to students' personal experiences or cultures.

- ✪ Conduct a class discussion in which students compare systems of measurement, learning about shapes, or other differences in math instruction they have experienced.

- ✪ Encourage students to share things they do at home that relate to what they are learning in math (e.g., planting a family garden, cooking or preparing a simple dish together, going to the store).

- ✪ Develop teaching materials that use this knowledge.

Cultural Differences

Different cultures use different sequences and approaches to teach math concepts. Many other cultures do not present math in a "spiral" framework, in which students are introduced to many concepts at very basic levels, and then each year instruction in all areas builds on that foundation.

For example, some countries do not introduce fractions or geometry until the upper elementary grades or later; young students may not comprehend and work with equal parts in the same way as students living in the United States or other English-speaking countries.

English Language Learner Instruction *(cont.)*
Skills for Math

Teach students the specific skills they need to complete activities and assignments. The skills provided on pp. 21–27 will help students in their understanding of math instruction.

Analyzing

Teach students this skill so they will examine problems more carefully. Breaking down multi-step problems into parts will help students understand how to solve problems.

Tips for Teaching the Skill

- ✪ Have students check to make sure they understand the words they are reading in directions.

- ✪ Have students analyze patterns to determine what comes next in the sequence.

- ✪ Ask students to tell what they have done, step by step, to solve a math problem.

- ✪ Help students learn to find their own mistakes and correct their work.

Sample Activity

Provide students with a sample problem, such as the following:

Yesterday it was 63 degrees outside. It is 92 degrees today. How much hotter is it today than yesterday? *(29 degrees)*

Tell students they do not need to think about finding the answer to the problem right away. Ask the class to list as many ways as they can think of to solve the problem. Discuss different strategies that might work. Have students explain the steps they would take, and the order in which they would do them, in order to solve the problem.

Clarifying

Teach students this skill so they can clarify meaning in math directions and problems. Encourage ELLs to stop and clarify when they read something they don't understand.

Tips for Teaching the Skill

- ✪ Ask questions and have students ask questions to help them clarify their thinking.

- ✪ Give students feedback on their responses to help students clarify their thinking.

- ✪ Invite students to explain to the class the math concept they just learned.

- ✪ Do comprehension checks to make sure that students understand the process for solving the problem.

- ✪ Help students distinguish the sounds and meanings between math words that sound similar (e.g., many, money; than, then).

- ✪ Create a poster or other visual reminder to help students understand math concepts, directions, and problems. Consider highlighting the following tips on your poster:

> ✔ Re-read.
>
> ✔ Look for visual cues.
>
> ✔ Check any unknown words.
>
> ✔ Read the context.

- ✪ Check in with individual English language learners after the lesson has been presented. Have them repeat back the assignment or review how to do the problem.

Sample Activity
Discuss with students and have them identify the steps needed to solve a problem; do not solve the problem, just focus on the language and meaning.

Classifying

Teach students this skill so they can learn to sort and group objects by their characteristics. Help students to classify objects by more than one attribute, such as shape, size, color, or texture.

Tips for Teaching the Skill

- ✪ Have students sort objects by various traits (e.g., recycling).

- ✪ Play a game in which children sort themselves by categories, such as who will eat a hot lunch and who will eat a cold lunch or colors of pants.

- ✪ Have students observe and discuss attributes of a common classroom item. Have them compare that item with another object in the classroom.

- ✪ Introduce and help students use words to describe the skill of classification, such as *some, all, part, pair, set, category*, and *different*.

- ✪ Encourage students to ask questions to help them classify objects.

Sample Activity
Collect all the students' shoes in a pile on the floor. Ask the class to brainstorm the different ways the shoes could be put into groups.

Comparing and Contrasting

Teach students this skill so they can compare and contrast groups of numbers and geometric shapes. Have students use this skill to understand how math problems are similar or different.

Tips for Teaching the Skill

- ✪ Use actual objects to help students learn to compare groups and determine which amount is more or less.

- ✪ Ask questions to help students learn the concept of "greater than" and "less than."

- ✪ Have students practice compare and contrast skills with patterns by finding patterns that are alike or different.

- ✪ Demonstrate and model for students how to compare and contrast in math class with numbers or other mathematical concepts, such as comparing shapes for congruency.

Sample Activity
Work together as a class to create an organizational chart to help students see the similarities and differences between different types of math sentences. Have students provide examples for *increase by, combine (addition), decrease by, find the difference, take away (subtraction)*, etc.

Making Connections

Teach students that they are making connections when they use what they already know to understand new math concepts. Encourage them to look for ways in which they use math in their daily lives.

Tips for Teaching the Skill

- ✪ Use manipulatives (pp. 28–29), such as buttons and beans, and drawings to help students understand concepts rather than just memorize steps in a process.

- ✪ Use concrete objects, pictures, diagrams, math symbols, and verbal expressions to help students remember mathematical concepts.

- ✪ Invite students to connect physical actions to counting and learning about numbers.

- ✪ Challenge students to make connections between the stories they read and the math concepts they have learned (e.g., shapes in illustrations or a numerical sequence in a story).

- ✪ Help students find a mathematical explanation when they do not understand how or why something works (e.g., how to make sure each child has an equal amount of time on the swings)

Sample Activity
Use mathematical language as students engage in various learning activities in the classroom. For example, when discussing pets, compare the amounts of food and water (using the appropriate measurement words) that each pet needs. Discuss how many minutes a pet plays or how often it needs to be walked.

English Language Learner Instruction (cont.)
Skills for Math (cont.)

Making Inferences

Teach students this skill so they can make accurate predictions, understand cause-and-effect relationships, and summarize information. Remind students that they make inferences when they use clues and what they already know about math processes to solve problems. Context clues such as explanations or details, along with students' background knowledge, can help students solve problems, make decisions, or answer questions.

Students make inferences in math when they do the following:

★ use their prior knowledge to understand what a problem is asking.

★ determine which information is most important in a problem.

★ use the information given to figure out the next step of a problem.

★ complete steps of a process in the proper order.

★ sequence events to understand problems.

Tips for Teaching the Skill

✪ Help students understand that they can understand what a problem is asking by studying context clues.

✪ Have students make predictions about what they think will happen when they manipulate objects to solve a math problem.

✪ Help students use what they already know to make decisions about which strategy or math operation to use when solving a problem.

Sample Activity
Create a graph displaying the favorite fruits (or vegetables) of students in the class. Explain that students use inference skills when they study information displayed in a graph to learn more about a group of people or objects. Have students use the graph to make inferences and answer questions, such as the following: • Which fruit did our class like most? • Which fruit did our class like least? • How many students liked apples? • How many students liked oranges? • Did more students like apples or oranges? • How many more students liked cherries than bananas?

Sequencing

Teach students this skill so they know how to create ordered lists of numbers, objects, or events. This is an important skill for students to learn, as many math problems require students to complete a series of steps in a specific order.

Tips for Teaching the Skill

- ✪ Use visual aids (pg. 50), mnemonic strategies (pg. 42), or peer tutoring (pg. 45) to help students remember the order of steps used to solve math problems.

- ✪ Have students sequence a series of events within the school day to learn about real time.

- ✪ Have students identify the steps they take—first, next, and last—to solve a problem or complete a problem-solving process.

Sample Activity
Have students practice sequencing various objects in the classroom. Challenge students to experiment with ordering by weight, length, number (e.g., number of linking cubes connected together), or other attributes. Invite students to create their own sequences and explain their sequences to partners. Set up timed buzz groups. Give students 5 minutes to work on a specific task, such as arranging picture cards in sequential order according to the time of day. At the end of 5 minutes, have groups share the ways they approached solving the problem. Follow up with questions about the order in which students do things during the school day.

Summarizing

Simply put, a summary briefly restates main points. Teach students that by highlighting numbers or keywords, they can focus on important details and the main point. Remind students that they summarize when they review, compile, or outline information.

Tips for Teaching the Skill

- ✪ Have students practice restating the main idea of a lesson in one or two sentences. Encourage students to use drawings to help them organize their thinking.

- ✪ Provide sentence frames for students to practice summarizing, such as "Today in math I learned that _____."

- ✪ Have students use summarizing to express the main ideas of word problems.

Sample Activity
Have students work with partners to summarize how to use the hour hand and the minute hand to tell time. Remind students that they will need to give their partners all the important information in just a few sentences. For example, a student might say, "The hour hand tells us what hour it is, and the minute hand tells us how many minutes it is past the hour."

English Language Learner Instruction *(cont.)*
Skills for Math *(cont.)*

Synthesizing

Teach students this skill so they know how to bring separate parts together into a whole. Learning this skill enables students to use what they know about math facts and principles to solve problems.

Tips for Teaching the Skill

- ✪ Help students connect main ideas to steps in a process so that they can see the parts of the whole.

- ✪ Provide opportunities for students to predict what will happen next in a series of events.

- ✪ Ask students how they could use math to solve a current problem in the classroom.

Sample Activity
Provide a variety of materials (e.g., dry beans, pictures of flowers) that students can use to create and extend patterns. Have pairs of students take turns predicting what comes next in their partners' patterns. Invite pairs to share their thinking as they created their patterns.

Visualizing

Teach students how to visualize so they can create math pictures in their minds. Students use their prior knowledge, known vocabulary, and understanding of math concepts to form mental images for problem solving and other math processes.

Tips for Teaching the Skill

- ✪ Ask students what they see in their minds when you read specific math terms.

- ✪ Use different kinds of pictures or graphics to help students understand math concepts, such as subtraction.

- ✪ Use color to help students visualize math facts and place value.

  - ★ Use a different color for each fact family. Have students write the 3s facts in orange, the 4s facts in green, the 5s facts in blue, etc.

  - ★ Use different colors to distinguish between ones and tens when learning place value.

- ✪ Help students visualize what is happening in a word problem by having them draw pictures to show their understanding of the situation described.

Sample Activity
Have students use visualization to identify geometric shapes within common classroom objects. Students will go on a scavenger hunt and then draw pictures or write the names of objects and the shapes noticed within the objects. (e.g., The cover of a book is a rectangle.)

English Language Learner Instruction (cont.)
Instructional Tools: Manipulatives

Manipulatives, real-world math examples (discrete mathematics, mathematization), and technology are three instructional tools that can increase student comprehension of math concepts. These tools are especially effective with kinesthetic, tactile, and visual learners—learners who often need to see, touch, and connect with objects in order to understand them.

Manipulatives enable students to think about and work with math before they have all the necessary language skills to express a given concept. As students express mathematical ideas with manipulatives, they increase their understanding of math problems and gain confidence in their math explorations.

Tips for Incorporating Manipulatives Into Math Curriculum

- ✪ Discuss with students how to use manipulatives and why they are important learning tools.

- ✪ Have students use manipulatives to demonstrate their learning.

- ✪ Help students use manipulatives to make connections to concepts and explanations presented in math textbooks.

- ✪ Use common objects as manipulatives (e.g., pencils, popcorn, pennies, small erasers). Create manipulatives using what's available.

- ✪ Have students use manipulatives to make real-life connections to math.

- ✪ Incorporate students' experiences with manipulatives into math writing assignments.

- ✪ Help students transition with manipulatives using the following diagram:

| concrete objects | ➡ | pictures | ➡ | symbols dots (sets), and number lines | ➡ | number sentences |

Types of Manipulative Materials

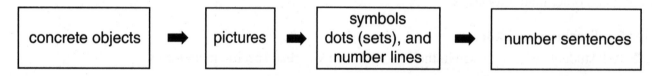

- counting chips
- tiles
- small blocks
- linking cubes
- attribute blocks
- laminated cardstock shapes

- buttons
- small crackers
- coins
- crayons or pencils
- dry beans
- picture/word cards for matching games (e.g., dominoes)

In the Classroom

Set up an organized system for storing manipulative materials and teach the system to students. Group manipulatives in one of the following ways:

- small bags for single-student use
- tubs for group use
- sorted by type for whole-class use

Allow time for students to explore materials before working on an assigned task.

Invite students to share their observations and discoveries with the class. Have students talk and write about what they have learned.

Create a class poster of manipulatives, if desired.

Teach students the names of the materials and post on charts as needed for future student reference.

At Home

Have students share their manipulative experiences with family members.

Allow students to borrow sample materials, using a check-out system, if desired.

Consider sending home a letter to parents describing the role that manipulatives have in math class.

Ask students to share with the class their use of manipulative materials at home.

Sample Activities

❂ Have students make word cards to list keywords for math operations. Cards can be cut to represent a theme or shape (e.g., The word *pentagon* could be written on a pentagon-shaped card.)

❂ Teach students about probability with the following real-life examples. Have students act out the scenarios and discuss what they learn about the results (draw conclusions).

★ Hana is coloring. She has crayons in a box next to the page. She cannot see inside the box. If there are eight different colored crayons in the box, what are the chances she will pull out the green crayon for the grass or the blue crayon for the sky? *(2-in-8 chance)* How likely is it that she will pull out any of the other six crayons? *(very likely)*

★ Chi likes green grapes the best. There is a bowl of eight cherries, four red grapes, six green grapes, and two pineapple chunks. How many pieces of fruit are in the bowl all together? *(20)* What are the chances he'll get a green grape? *(6-in-20 chance)*

Discrete mathematics uses real-world examples to connect math concepts to everyday life. It helps students apply math and make it relevant to real life. These types of math lessons include concrete, visual, and hands-on strategies, which provide additional support for English language learners.

Students at all grade levels use discrete mathematics principles and applications, such as systematic listing and counting, vertex-edge graphs, and iteration (repeating patterns or steps in a process) as they learn and practice math. Use the principles of discrete mathematics to encourage students to find solutions to real-life problems.

Systematic Listing and Counting

Students practice this skill when they sort objects by attributes, categorize information, or determine how many combinations of different objects can be formed.

Sample Activities

✪ Have students sort and list items (e.g., fruit or crackers) that members of the class have in their lunches. Students can use the information to make graphs and make predictions about future student lunches, plan class events, or analyze data to learn about classmates.

✪ Have students identify and count the items each group will need for a specific task, such as a social studies, science, or art project.

✪ Provide a selection of nickels and dimes for students. Explain that this money is a class set for learning purposes. Ask students to arrange the coins to determine how many different ways they can make $1.00 (or 50¢, if that is more appropriate for your students). Create a story context applicable for your students, if desired. Even though this is a common classroom activity, it introduces the concept of making combinations with real-life objects, gives students experience with American money, and reinforces counting by 5s and 10s.

Vertex-Edge Graphs

Students use the concept of a vertex-edge graph when they color a map of the United States with four colors so that the same two colors do not touch each other. This is called four-color map theory. Students develop graphing skills when they find the best way to get from point A to point B or the closest location to a given point.

Sample Activities

✪ Create a vertex-edge graph from a simple map. Draw a vertex inside each region or area of the map. Draw lines to connect the vertices that are in regions that share a border. (These are edges.) Remove the map to see the graph that represents it. As a class, create such a map to discuss the most efficient route from the school to the park or how many different routes students can take to get from the hospital to the library.

English Language Learner Instruction *(cont.)*
Instructional Tools: Discrete Mathematics *(cont.)*

Vertex-Edge Graphs *(cont.)*

Sample Activities *(cont.)*

- ✪ Explore the concept of four-color theory when dividing students into reading groups. Display a copy of the class-seating chart. Work together to assign each student one of four colors in such a way that no two colors are next to each other. If desired, give students tokens representing their assigned colors to help students remember their colors. Students will be able to group themselves during the transition to reading time as they go to their color group areas. Whenever groups need to change or the class needs to group themselves for other content-area activities, have the students practice four-color theory.

Iteration

This area of discrete mathematics refers to the repetition of patterns or actions in a process. Students practice this skill not only when they work with patterns but also when they repeat actions in a process to reach a goal. Provide opportunities for students to use patterns to solve problems.

Sample Activities

- ✪ Have volunteers share when they did an action over and over again to complete a task. Ask questions about the experiences to investigate and extend the patterns. Transfer the questions and answers into mathematical symbols and number sentences. Draw pictures first to describe the patterns as needed.

- ✪ Ask students to line up in different ways, using various patterns (e.g., number order, patterns of girls and boys, colors of shirts or shoes).

English Language Learner Instruction *(cont.)*
Instructional Tools: Mathematization

Introduce students to the concept of "mathematization," or finding math in everyday experiences and expressing it in math terms. Relate math to other topics of study, such as quilt or wallpaper designs (geometric shapes), maps and travel (measurement), sports (time), architecture (angles, measurement), sales advertisements (money), and bus schedules (time).

The following sample activities, which are organized by category, will help your students make connections between math and the real world.

Operations	Ask students to think of their favorite meals. Then have them list all of the ingredients and amounts. Ask them to total the number of ingredients. Then tell them that guests are coming, so they'll need to double the servings. How will this change the number of ingredients and amounts? What if two guests come? Or three? Choose the option(s) most appropriate for your students' language levels.
Geometry	Take the class for a walk outside. Have them observe and document what geometric shapes are seen in nature and around school. Discuss with students the games they like to play. Have them think about what shapes are included in the games (e.g., dice are cubes, checkerboards have squares, cards are rectangular). Have examples on hand to share with the class.
Measurement and Estimation	Have students estimate, calculate, and measure when making models in science or social studies. Practice measuring ingredients for "no-bake" recipes or to create substances to investigate in science. Have students measure classroom items for a useful purpose (e.g., to make name tags or to create a bulletin board display).
Money	Discuss and role-play how to compare prices and use mental math. Set up a class store with realia, or real-life items. Keep an assortment of coins in your pocket and randomly ask students to count money or answer simple questions individually during student work time.

Use technology—such as software, demonstration videos, interactive sites, and computer games—to help ELLs construct math knowledge. Because students are already familiar with these resources, the math concepts provided seem less foreign and more understandable.

Software

Go beyond software that offers basic math practice and incorporate simulation software that introduces students to real-life counting activities or arithmetic operations.

Sample Activities

Have students use a paint program to design sets of objects for partners to count and classify.

Use clip art to create a sample store flier with appropriate prices for students to practice adding and subtracting money in a real-world setting.

Demonstration Videos

Use cameras and other audiovisual equipment to record videos that portray teachers and students completing math problems and engaging in other math-related activities.

Sample Activity

Use the record feature on an interactive whiteboard to document a series of steps for a procedure, such as shading a fractional part and then writing the corresponding fraction number or completing a multi-step word problem with addition or subtraction.

Interactive Math Sites

These sites provide many resources for teachers, including games for practicing specific math skills, activities for interactive whiteboards, and math investigations. See "Websites for Educators" (pp. 108–109) for a list of recommended math sites.

Sample Activity

Use interactive math sites to post a problem of the week for the class, or have students observe patterns or explore a simple math glossary.

Computer Games

Computer games can help students practice critical-thinking skills, increase their confidence with and exposure to math concepts, and give them opportunities to use problem-solving skills. When computer games are one factor among many in a classroom that employs diverse teaching and learning strategies, some students may improve their scores on standardized testing.

Sample Activities

Have students solve addition and subtraction problems to decode secret messages using math words.

Play Hangman or another vocabulary game on an interactive whiteboard to introduce students to new math vocabulary.

English Language Learner Instruction *(cont.)*
Teaching Strategies

Teachers use a variety of techniques, methods, and materials to help their ELLs meet learning goals and objectives. The strategies provided in this section may help students feel at ease in the classroom, participate in lessons, and learn new content at the same time they are learning a new language. Incorporate a variety of teaching strategies into lesson plans and classroom activities to address students' needs.

Asking Questions

Use this strategy to help students identify specific information. Questions engage students as they take ownership of their learning. Asking questions, such as "why" or "how," helps students to develop their critical-thinking skills. Model how to ask questions so that students understand question structure and question-word meaning. Encourage students to ask questions when solving problems. Then relate those questions to the main math concept in the lesson.

Examples

gesture-eliciting questions—Show me which pile of seeds has more seeds.

yes/no questions—Do you have any green seeds?

short-answer questions—Are there more smooth seeds or rough seeds?

sentence frames—You found the number of brown seeds by _____.

Tips for Teaching the Strategy

★ Structure questions so that students will respond.

★ Begin with questions that students can respond to with gestures.

★ Break questions into parts. Use shorter sentences.

★ Ask questions to engage students and help them take the next step in their thinking as they explore a math topic.

★ Ask questions that require students to explain their thinking.

★ Offer questions at various proficiency levels for English language learners.

★ Practice wait time. Students need time for the following:

  • to process questions.

  • to solve problems and answer questions.

  • to complete assignments.

Sample Activity

Have students graph a variety of seeds that might be used to plant a garden. Ask students questions at different levels of English proficiency that are similar to the examples above. Differentiate questions based on students' abilities, progressing from simple questions about numbers of different colors of seeds to comparing categories of seeds and solving problems based on the data they compile about their seeds.

English Language Learner Instruction *(cont.)*
Teaching Strategies *(cont.)*

Brainstorming

Use this strategy to activate students' prior knowledge or help them think about how to solve math problems. Have students think of as many answers to a question or ways to approach a math problem as possible, and then write down everyone's ideas. Teach students brainstorming techniques so that they develop their problem-solving skills.

Examples: webs, lists (e.g., ways to use math tools), clustering (about a concept), diagrams, mind maps, word associations, K-W-L charts, categorizing information (e.g., group related ideas), asking questions (pg. 34), discussing strategies with classmates, drawing pictures to generate ideas

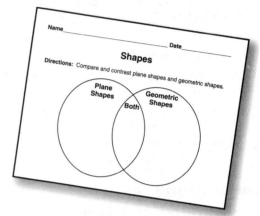

Tips for Teaching the Strategy

★ When compiling students' input, make sure everyone can see the diagram.

★ Encourage all students to participate. Model respect for all contributors.

★ Consider a small motivational incentive to encourage ELLs to participate in sharing their ideas aloud.

Sample Activities

Have students brainstorm different approaches to solving calendar-related problems. Encourage students to demonstrate for classmates how they solved problems (e.g., counting forward, counting back, counting number of days in a month, drawing a picture). Generate a class list or web of problem-solving ideas for future reference.

Many countries use decimal points and commas differently than English-speaking countries. After teaching students the difference, have them compare and contrast commas and decimal points.

Have students think of as many ways to solve problems as possible and write down everyone's ideas. Pose the question "What would happen if . . . ?" to help students get started.

Have students brainstorm ways math relates to the real world and how they use math in their everyday lives.

English Language Learner Instruction *(cont.)*
Teaching Strategies *(cont.)*

Graphic Organizers

Use this strategy to organize information, explain relationships between words, and help students see connections between ideas. Model for students how to use a graphic organizer so that they can connect new content to prior learning in meaningful ways.

Examples: word webs, semantic maps, compare and contrast diagrams (e.g., Venn diagrams), sequence charts, grids, organizational charts, T-charts, pictograph charts, bar graphs, number lines

Tips for Teaching the Strategy

* Adapt graphic organizers to match ELLs' levels of proficiency in English.

* Use semantic webs to help students understand parts of a whole concept, such as types of numbers, or to categorize concepts, such as tools and units for measurement.

Sample Activity

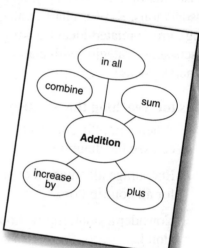

Use webs to help students understand how different math terms relate to each other or sometimes mean the same thing. Write the word *add* (or *addition)* in the center circle and invite students to think of other words and phrases that describe the same process in the outer circles. To create a similar web for subtraction, include the following terms: *subtract* (center circle), *decreased by, take away, minus, less than, fewer,* and *difference.*

Interactive Activities

Use this teaching strategy to motivate students and address multiple learning styles as students participate directly in the lesson. Students test their ideas and are exposed to different ways of thinking about math when they participate in activities with other people or a variety of materials. Introduce activities and integrate techniques that encourage interaction, such as incorporating math concepts into art projects, assigning quick-writes, or instructing students to survey classmates for a data collection and graphing exercise.

Examples

Dialogue Journals

Have students exchange pictures labeled with words or sentences back and forth with partners, the teacher, or another adult aide or mentor. Assign various math topics for discussion.

Guided Lecture

1. Present the new information or math concept.

2. Invite students to share at least one question or comment about what they heard.

3. Write students' questions and comments on chart paper, a whiteboard, or an interactive whiteboard.

4. Review student notes with the class to check understanding.

5. Divide students into small groups (pg. 47). Assign one question or comment to each small group and have students discuss it in the context of the new math concept.

Interactive Lecture

Have students actively listen to the lesson. As they listen, they will do the following four things: (1) think, (2) stop, (3) draw a picture or symbol and/or write one or more words, and (4) give feedback to partners or to the teacher. Invite students to share and explain their drawings and words that they chose to write. Have students ask questions to clarify what they heard and to help them develop their listening skills.

Interest Groups

Have all students work on mastering the same concept (e.g., practicing estimation) with different types of problems that are based on ability and interest level (estimating distance, amount of objects in a set, money, etc.)

Pictorial Representations

Show students a graphic representation, such as a diagram or drawing, of a math concept. Do not include any words or explanations. Ask students to identify and explain the concept or problem-solving process represented. If desired, have students draw and label pictures to demonstrate their understanding of the concept using terms they have already learned.

Quick-Write

1. Pose a problem or a question.

2. Have students draw and write their answers.

3. Ask students to share their responses with the class.

4. Discuss the (different) strategies students used to solve the problem.

Interactive Activities *(cont.)*

Shared Input

Talk for 5 minutes, then do a think-pair-share activity (pg. 49) for 2 minutes, then have students share as a class for 2 minutes.

Sketch to Solve

Teach students a series of steps to solve problems.

1. Sketch a picture or diagram.

2. Select an operation (addition, subtraction, counting, dividing, or grouping objects in a set).

3. Set up a number sentence.

4. Find the answer to the number sentence.

5. Check to see if the solution makes sense.

Triangle Groups

1. Divide students into groups of three.

2. Have the first student read a math problem.

3. The next student will circle important numbers and underline the problem question.

4. Have the third student guide and lead a discussion among group members about how to solve the problem.

Tips for Teaching the Strategy

★ Pair native English speakers with ELL students to give them opportunities to hear different explanations.

★ Encourage students to ask each other questions.

★ Create simple games or adapt trade games, such as Tic-Tac-Toe, Concentration, or Hide-and-Seek, to practice specific math skills or concepts.

★ Teach students routines for caring for materials and cleaning up when activities are finished.

Sample Activities

Help students develop one-to-one counting skills, visual number sense, and comparison (greater than, less than) skills by playing a game similar to "Around the World." Hold a different number of marbles or other small counters in each hand. Open both hands at the same time and have students point to the hand that holds the greatest number of counters. Students may or may not compete against partners.

Use a count-and-capture game such as Mancala to help students practice one-on-one counting and planning-ahead strategies. (With Mancala, students can play in pairs; draw the playing board on paper, and use any small counters of which you have several per pair of students.)

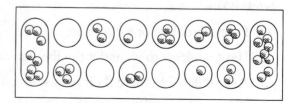

English Language Learner Instruction *(cont.)*

Teaching Strategies *(cont.)*

Marking Text

Use this strategy to teach students how to mark text, or make notations, as they read. Marking text allows students to interact with what they read, increasing their comprehension. In a visual subject such as math, marking text helps students form mental pictures of what the problem is asking and develop appropriate strategies to find the solution. This strategy helps students do the following:

- ✪ comprehend what they read.
- ✪ notice patterns.
- ✪ identify what the problem is asking.
- ✪ identify relevant information needed to solve the problem.

Examples

underlining—emphasizing keywords, key phrases, or examples

highlighting—coloring specific vocabulary words and defining them in the margins

circling—emphasizing examples

sticky notes—tabbing pages, especially to mark equations or formulas often used

colors—using highlighters, crayons, or colored pencils to identify parts of a problem or different numerical operations within a problem

letters/symbols—coding parts of a word problem, including what the question is asking, relevant details or information, and irrelevant or unnecessary information

Tips for Teaching the Strategy

- ★ Give students a purpose for marking text.
- ★ Model different ways of marking text, showing students explicitly how to use this strategy.
- ★ Consider making photocopies of a text or math problem so that students can mark freely.
- ★ Use clear plastic sheets over textbook pages or practice test booklets with washable markers.
- ★ Use scanners, document cameras, or interactive whiteboard technology to project copies of text.
- ★ Have all teachers use the same ways of marking text to provide consistency across grade levels or between leveled math classes.

Sample Activities

Have students use different colors to represent the following questions:

- • What do I know?
- • What is the problem asking?
- • Have I seen this type of problem before?

English Language Learner Instruction *(cont.)*
Teaching Strategies *(cont.)*

Marking Text *(cont.)*

Sample Activities *(cont.)*

Many students have difficulty extracting the correct data from story problems. Teach students how to identify the relevant information and differentiate it from the irrelevant. Use the following problem as an example. Have students mark the relevant text in one color and the irrelevant text in another color. Students may also need to circle keywords and numbers to create an appropriate number sentence or equation.

> This morning when we came into the classroom, the outside temperature was 42 degrees. The sun came out, and now it is 61 degrees. Yesterday morning it was 57 degrees. How much warmer did it get between yesterday morning and this morning?
> *(57 degrees – 42 degrees = 15 degrees)*

Help students identify and circle the key numbers 42 and 57. Help students recognize that "The sun came out, and now it is 61 degrees" is irrelevant information and should be marked a different color.

Display and provide copies of a math text passage. Read the passage together as a class. Think aloud to show students how to code it with symbols, such as the following:

✔ I already knew this.

* This is new to me.

? I have a question.

Have students read the passage on their own or with partners and make their own marks regarding their understanding of the reading. Call on volunteers to share how and why they marked the passage.

English Language Learner Instruction *(cont.)*
Teaching Strategies *(cont.)*

Math Journals

Use this strategy to help students make sense of new concepts and ideas in math. Students can use writing to think through the step-by-step processes of solving particular math problems. Start by having students describe how they solved a particular problem. Write what students say. Then progress to math-concept reflections, learning summaries, and free-writing prompts.

Ways to Use Math Journals

- Have students complete daily problems in their journals.

- Ask students to write one journal entry at the end of class to reflect on the day's learning. (A journal entry may be only a sentence or two.)

- Encourage students to use their journals to ask questions they have.

- Have students write what they have learned about a math concept in a journal entry.

- Have students use their journals for review.

- Encourage students to include sketches, drawings, diagrams, and labels in their journals to think about how to solve math problems.

Tips for Teaching the Strategy

- ★ Allow students to use their native languages in their math journals.

- ★ Communicate your expectations for and model how students should write in their journals.

- ★ Give students sentence stems to help them start writing about math.

- ★ Have students verbalize a sentence or two to a teacher, aide, or classmate, then write down what they just said. Continue this process to help students feel more comfortable with writing their thoughts.

- ★ Use prompts to guide students as they reflect on what they are thinking, feeling, and doing in math class.

- ★ Use a specific journal prompt to conduct a class discussion. Writing their responses before sharing in class will help ELLs clarify their thinking in English.

- ★ Allow ELLs to draw and label pictures and then verbally explain their pictures.

- ★ Refer to words posted on a word wall to use in free-writing prompts.

- ★ As time allows, give students written feedback on selected journal entries.

Sample Activity

Provide students with a math problem, based on a current class read-aloud story, to reflect on and solve in their math journals. After students have practiced with sample problems from the same story for two or three class sessions, challenge students to think of their own problems based on the story. Have them write the problems in their math journals to share with partners to solve.

Mnemonic Strategies

Use this strategy to help students remember new information. Mnemonic strategies are most often auditory or verbal but may also be visual or kinesthetic. They may include keywords and/or illustrations to help students remember a series of words or facts. Here are the steps to implementing mnemonic strategies:

1. Provide students with the mnemonic device you want them to use.

2. Demonstrate and explain how to use the strategy to remember a particular fact or concept.

3. Practice with students to help them use the strategy correctly.

Examples: keywords, names, rhymes, poems, pictures, number chants or songs

Tip for Teaching the Strategy

Make sure students understand the basic concepts before teaching a mnemonic device.

Sample Activities

Provide rhyming words to help students learn number words.

Use pictures of bicycles (or cars) to help students learn the +2 (or +4) fact family. Students add the number of wheels as pictures are added to the discussion.

Models

Use this strategy to help explain or describe math concepts to students. Have students use manipulative materials to create models, or representations, of math problems. Students can use these models to understand arithmetic operations, fractions, or geometric properties.

Examples: fraction pieces, base-10 blocks, pattern blocks, drawings, graphs

Tips for Teaching the Strategy

★ Draw basic shapes to represent parts of a situation described in a word problem.

★ Use blocks to build a model that shows what is happening in a word problem.

★ Have students become living models in a role-playing exercise.

Sample Activity

Have students role-play the following problem. They can draw four place settings on paper and repurpose used, crumpled-up scraps of paper for the meatballs. Then have students extend the role-play with other family meal scenarios.

> Jalea helps her mom with dinner. Tonight they will eat meatballs. There are four people in Jalea's family. Her mom cooked twelve meatballs. How many meatballs will each person eat? (*3 meatballs*)

English Language Learner Instruction *(cont.)*
Teaching Strategies *(cont.)*

Multisensory Activities

Use this strategy to engage students in nonverbal ways. Multisensory activities enable teachers to adapt lessons for different student learning styles.

Examples

Visual	Auditory
Create math problems from photographs. Use multimedia presentations to demonstrate math concepts. Use color to highlight specific parts of a math concept (e.g., place value). Use video clips to illustrate real-life word problems.	Introduce chants. Incorporate songs. Use mnemonic strategies (pg. 42). Read aloud stories about math concepts. Use an interactive whiteboard to associate sounds with keywords. (e.g., Use a different sound for each coin to help students learn coin values.)
Kinesthetic	**Tactile**
Incorporate movement. (e.g., Have students act out problems.) Encourage air writing. Play catch while reviewing math facts.	Use magnets. Explore geometric shapes created from textured surfaces, such as fabric and sand paper. Sort objects by attributes.

Tips for Teaching the Strategy

★ Try to involve more than one sense in a math lesson.

★ Present word problems using multisensory activities.

Sample Activity

Have students estimate (guess and check) and then weigh fruit or other snack items. The smell and feel of various items as students record weights in standard (or nonstandard) units will give them a frame of reference for subsequent classroom activities in estimating and measurement.

Numbered Heads

Use this strategy so students can work together in groups to discuss a new concept or solve a problem. Here are the steps to the numbered heads strategy:

1. Assign each student a number.

2. Put students into small groups. Each group should have a complete set of numbers represented. (If students have been given numbers 1, 2, and 3, then there should be three students to a group— one with number 1, one with number 2, and one with number 3.)

3. Give groups a problem. Allow them time to discuss the problem and solution(s).

4. After students have worked together to ensure that everyone in the group understands, randomly call a specific number to indicate which student in each group should share with the whole class. (Decide prior to the activity whether or not you want the person who shares to have the option of receiving help from the group when sharing.)

5. If a problem has only one correct answer, have other teams in the class use a simple signal to indicate whether they agree or disagree with the given answer.

Ways to Use Numbered Heads: when teaching word problems, learning and discussing new math terms, discussing shapes and attributes, reviewing for a test or quiz

Tips for Teaching the Strategy

★ Select three volunteers to help you model for the class how to work together to make sure everyone in the group fully understands the problem or concept (without anyone giving other students the answer).

★ Use the "roll the dice" feature on an interactive whiteboard to randomly select which student number shares.

Sample Activity

Provide groups with manipulatives to explore measurement. Have students work together to understand how many cups are in a pint, how many pints are in a quart, etc.

English Language Learner Instruction (cont.)
Teaching Strategies (cont.)

Peer Tutoring

Use this strategy to train students in instructional methods so they can help one another. Peer tutoring should be used with content that has already been taught in class. Have one partner "teach" the material and give feedback to the other. At a signal, partners switch roles.

Ways to Use Peer Tutoring

- Tell your students to be aware of when their partners start to have trouble.

- Have partners repeat back to check for understanding.

- Instruct students to explain how to find the answer.

- Remind students to not give the answers directly to their partners.

- Tell students to create an explanation of how to do the problem.

- Have students use drawings or manipulative objects (pp. 28–29).

- Make sure that each tutoring partnership is appropriate and beneficial. Use the table below as a guide.

Need	Tutor	Tutee
translate, learn new vocabulary	ELL student—same proficiency level	ELL student—same proficiency level
translate, learn new vocabulary, ask questions to give partners experience explaining answers	highly skilled	less skilled
assistance learning English	native English speaker	ELL student
learn new math skills, ask questions to give partners experience explaining answers	higher-grade-level student	lower-grade-level student

Tips for Teaching the Strategy

★ Use peer tutoring to help students learn number operations, vocabulary, number concepts, measurement, or fractions.

★ Identify one learning objective and review with the class to help students focus on the task at hand.

★ Give tutors prompts to use.

Sample Activity

Provide data for students to create a pictograph. Students can help each other create the graph and then ask each other questions about the graph to meet a stated learning objective, such as "Collects and represents information about objects or events in simple graphs" (Standard 6, Benchmark 1).

English Language Learner Instruction (cont.)
Teaching Strategies (cont.)

Sentence Frames

Use this strategy to provide structure for students learning academic language. Sentence frames—also called sentence starters, sentence stems, or communication guides—have one or more keywords left blank in a sentence. Use sentence frames to do the following:

- ✪ help students learn new vocabulary in context.
- ✪ introduce complex math concepts.
- ✪ help students talk about math.
- ✪ help students understand word problems.

Use the following steps when using sentence frames to help students understand word problems:

1. Read a sentence frame aloud.
2. Have students repeat the sentence.
3. Clarify to ensure that everyone understands all the words.
4. Model saying the sentence aloud again.
5. Ask why the sentence might or might not be true.
6. Have students fill in their own numbers, symbols, or words to make the sentence true.

Examples: "_____ and _____ are _____ (even/odd) numbers";

"I know that _____ is an _____ (even/odd) number because _____";

"_____ *(Odd)* numbers cannot be divided evenly into _____ *(groups)* of two."

Tips for Teaching the Strategy

- ★ Use sentence frames to teach students to use complete sentences when talking about math.
- ★ Ask yourself what you want students to be able to say about a particular math concept, and then develop a sentence frame to help them communicate their understanding.
- ★ Have students share their completed sentence frames with partners or small groups to check for accuracy.
- ★ Create sentence frames based on real-world scenarios.

Sample Activity

Provide a series of math-related sentence frames. Work together as a class to complete the sentences. Say the first sentence aloud and then have students repeat. Continue with all the sentences. Challenge students to create chants or rhymes to help them remember what they have learned. Have students continue to practice with variations of the original sentence(s).

English Language Learner Instruction *(cont.)*
Teaching Strategies *(cont.)*

Small Groups

Use this strategy to help decrease student anxiety and increase motivation. Small groups allow students to ask questions and receive feedback in an environment of positive support. In small groups, students can receive explanations from classmates, which may be easier for them to understand. Have students work in pairs or small groups of three or more.

The small-groups strategy teaches students group interaction skills, such as the following:

- ✪ how to work through conflicts.
- ✪ how to manage time well.
- ✪ how to contribute to the group (in one or more ways).

Examples: mixed-language groups; mixed-ability groups; homogenous groups in which students work on a particular skill; groups in which students role-play, solve a problem, complete a task, or brainstorm ideas

Tips for Teaching the Strategy

- ★ Before giving students a content-area task, have them practice their group social interaction skills with an icebreaker activity.
- ★ Have students rotate from one group to another periodically.

Sample Activity

Pose a problem-solving activity, such as the one below. Provide manipulative objects (e.g., fraction pieces) to solve the problem. Assign roles to group members as follows:

Reader—reads the math problem to the group

Manipulatives Manager—finds or gathers objects to actively demonstrate the problem

Artist—draws pictures to illustrate the problem

Writer—writes a number sentence using numbers and symbols

Speaker—explains how the group arrived at an answer

> Dana's softball team had a pizza party with two pizzas. One-half of the cheese pizza was left over. One-fourth of the pepperoni pizza was left over. Did the team eat more cheese pizza or more pepperoni pizza? *(pepperoni pizza)*

English Language Learner Instruction (cont.)
Teaching Strategies (cont.)

Think-Alouds

Use this strategy to show students how to think through the problem-solving process. In doing so, you model the steps needed to solve a problem. Encourage students to use think-alouds when reviewing concepts. Students can use what they know to help them reflect on how to solve new problems. Thinking aloud will help students remember the steps in a process and the order in which to do the steps.

Ways to Use Think-Alouds: when working arithmetic algorithms, solving word problems

Tip for Teaching the Strategy

Have students work with partners and take turns creating similar problems (using different numbers or objects).

Sample Activity

Write the following problem on the board. Tell students that even though this problem does not have any numbers, they will need to think through several steps to solve the problem. Read the problem aloud, and think aloud to talk through how it could be solved.

> Ben is shorter than Rob but taller than James. James is taller than Dan. Which of these four boys is the tallest?

Possible thoughts: When I first read this problem, I just hear a bunch of names. How can I sort out all these people? I know what the words *shorter* and *taller* mean, but here I am comparing more than two people, and that makes it confusing. I'll look away from the problem and try to retell what I just read.

All I can remember is that the boys' names are Rob, James, and Dan. Check me and see how much I remember. Oops, I didn't even remember the fourth boy's name! And I certainly don't know who is taller or shorter than the others. I need to read this out loud again. Now I'll read it over again to myself. This will be the third time I read the problem. We'll see how much I can remember now when I try to tell it back to you.

Let's see, I know now that Ben is shorter than one of the others. James is taller than one of the others. I want to figure out who is the tallest person.

Did I remember more that time? Yes, I got Ben in the right position as being shorter than someone and James in the right position as being taller than someone. I remembered that I need to find the tallest person. Given the information I can remember, how would I state this problem in my own words?

Ben is shorter than Rob. James is taller than Dan. Ben is taller than James. Who is the tallest? *(Rob)*

Does that help? What can I do to try to solve this problem? I could draw stick people with four different heights. Then I could try to name the people. I'd better use a pencil and an eraser or a whiteboard because I might have to erase and try again! I can write the names under the people, and if it doesn't work, I'll erase and try the names under different figures.

English Language Learner Instruction *(cont.)*
Teaching Strategies *(cont.)*

Think-Pair-Share

Use this strategy so ELLs can rehearse what they want to say, negotiate meaning with partners, and expand or correct their understanding. Here are the steps to think-pair-share:

1. Pose a question or problem for students to think about.

2. Give students a set amount of time to think (e.g., one or two minutes). Encourage students to just think about how they would solve the problem. Have students write their responses before sharing, if desired.

3. Pair up students to discuss and develop their ideas. Time students again as they take turns sharing with partners.

4. Call on a few students to share their responses with the class.

Ways to Use Think-Pair-Share: reviewing a new topic, brainstorming (pg. 35) how to solve a problem, summarizing (pg. 26) what a word problem is asking

Tips for Teaching the Strategy

★ Assign partners at the beginning of the lesson.

★ Have students take turns sharing with each other. Use a timer, if necessary.

★ Change partners for different lessons.

Sample Activities

Have students discuss with their partners which strategy they would use to solve a problem and why. Then have students solve the problem on their own. Students may then share their answers with their partners.

Have students discuss with partners how to round numbers or how to determine place value.

English Language Learner Instruction (cont.)
Teaching Strategies (cont.)

Visual Aids

Use this strategy to help students solve problems while supporting students' language development. Visual aids can help students focus on reasoning and problem-solving skills. Use visual aids to help students clarify meaning and relate new vocabulary and concepts to graphic representations.

Examples: charts, diagrams, graphs, pictures, video clips, gestures, posters, flash cards, word lists

Tips for Teaching the Strategy

★ Use visual aids to restate the main idea of a lesson.

★ Use clip art or simple line drawings from the Internet to illustrate various math problems and concepts.

★ Encourage students to use visual aids as a way to remember key math concepts.

Sample Activities

Use objects to demonstrate solid geometrical shapes, such as dice to represent a cube, an ice-cream cone to represent a cone, and a small bouncy ball to represent a sphere.

Use real objects for graphing activities (e.g., the number of buttons on students' clothing).

Whole-Group Response

Use this strategy to emphasize particular points or review information. Whole-group response also provides opportunities for informal assessment during class. Have students respond together as a group verbally, in writing, or with movement.

This strategy is also helpful for struggling ELLs who are less inclined to answer independently. In answering with their peers, ELLs feel less pressure and are more likely to participate.

Examples: flash cards; response or answer cards; individual whiteboards; interactive whiteboard personal response systems; gestures, such as thumbs up or thumbs down; physical movements, such as standing up or sitting down; chants

Tip for Teaching the Strategy

Start by having students echo back a word or phrase to learn new vocabulary and pronunciation of math terms.

Sample Activity

Provide answer cards or have students make their own. Students may have more than one card to respond to a series of questions, such as the correct place value of a two- or three-digit number or whether a number is even or odd.

Math Language Connections
Vocabulary

Math introduces students to new vocabulary, terms, phrases, and sentence structures. Understanding these math language connections helps students think about math and comprehend new concepts.

Vocabulary instruction includes teaching students math-specific definitions of words, as well as how to use the new math vocabulary they are learning. Learning the language structures used in math will help students experience success in other academic areas as well.

Tips for Teaching Math Vocabulary

✪ Provide language acquisition support to help students learn new math terms.

✪ Use students' primary languages when possible to teach math terms and make connections to English.

✪ Allow students to explain mathematical ideas and concepts to one another in their native languages.

✪ Have students repeat vocabulary words back. Check for correct pronunciations.

✪ Teach students the difference between "tens" and "tenths." Many ELLs have trouble with the "th" sound.

✪ Introduce vocabulary with descriptions and examples. Use the "Glossary: Math Terms" (pp. 54–60) and "Glossary: Math Verbs" (pp. 61–62) as guides.

✪ Teach math-specific definitions for common multiple-meaning math terms (e.g., *quarter, point, table, left*).

✪ Paraphrase new math vocabulary and model how to use it when teaching new concepts.

✪ Have students use new words in contextual sentences so they can talk about math concepts.

✪ Give students multiple exposures to new words.

✪ Teach word parts, as appropriate.

✪ Teach sentence patterns through explanations and examples.

✪ Provide relevant examples when teaching new terms and concepts.

✪ Use visual cues, graphic representations, gestures, objects, and pictures when teaching new vocabulary.

✪ Use graphic organizers to provide context as students learn academic language.

✪ Scaffold students by creating a context for new vocabulary. For example, demonstrate—with fixed classroom objects (e.g., walls, floor), manipulatives, or pictures—the meaning of "between."

✪ Create word walls or charts with commonly used terms for student reference. Organize word walls so students can easily access the terms they need. Students can focus on math processes and learn the terms through practice.

Math Language Connections (cont.)
Vocabulary (cont.)

Actions to Improve Students' Vocabulary

The chart below includes actions that teachers and students can execute in order to improve students' vocabulary.

What Teachers Can Do	What Students Can Do
Use explicit instruction to teach new vocabulary each day. Include the following steps: Incorporate vocabulary activities into math lessons. Pre-teach keywords and key phrases. Help students learn to talk about math. Offer opportunities for student practice that leads to independence. Include linguistic and nonlinguistic representations of terms. Help students associate new vocabulary words with mental pictures, sounds, touch, or even smells or tastes. Provide synonyms to connect key concepts with important vocabulary words. Use math journals to give students opportunities to practice writing new math words. Have students practice new vocabulary in class. (e.g., Ask questions using new vocabulary and model how to answer using the new word. Provide sentence frames, if necessary.)	Take a multi-step approach to learning vocabulary, which includes the following: Discuss and play with math language. Compare and classify groups of vocabulary words. Practice using new words in cloze activities and then compose sentences of their own with the words. Restate new terms or phrases in their own words. Identify the ways in which new words are used in daily math lessons. Share definitions and understandings with partners. Look at graphics and create captions for them. Listen to new words read aloud. Write or draw personal connections to new words. Practice using vocabulary with word maps. Participate in cooperative group learning activities.

Math Vocabulary Activities

✪ Ask questions throughout the school day that incorporate math concepts. Consider sharing the following lunch examples:

  ⋆ How many students have cold lunches today?

  ⋆ How many more students have hot lunches than cold lunches?

✪ Observe changes in the classroom and restate those changes as math problems. Consider re-enacting the following activity:

  ⋆ Rearrange specific objects in the classroom. Conduct a class discussion about what has changed, using specific words to describe spatial relationships and time. For example, "The reading table was next to the door. Now it is by the bookcase." "There were 4 chairs at the table. Now there are 6. There are 2 more chairs at the table today than yesterday."

✪ Invite students to discuss how they use math during other times of the school day or after school.

✪ Post vocabulary cards on various math-related objects around the room. Go from object to object, asking students (as a class or individually) to say the names on the cards. Check for correct pronunciations.

✪ Help students practice their pronunciation of ordinal and cardinal numbers. Draw a simple table with two columns and several rows on the board. Write cardinal and ordinal numbers in each cell of the chart in random order. Include numbers as well as number words, if desired. Read one word at a time from each row and ask students to show with fingers if you are reading a word from the first column or the second column. For instance, when you read the word "tenth," students should show two fingers to indicate you read a word from the second column.

#1	#2
ten	tenth
sixths	six
tenths	tens
eight	eighth
hundred	hundredth
hundredth	hundreds

Once you've gone through both columns, have students say the words as a class. Check for correct pronunciations.

✪ Start a word map that students can finish. Include one or several of the following: a definition, examples and non-examples, other forms of the word, visual examples, and when you might use the word. Word maps help students think about and develop their understanding of new words and concepts.

Math Language Connections *(cont.)*
Glossary: Math Terms

Math has its own jargon—a vocabulary that can be tricky for struggling ELLs who are still learning the fundamentals of English. ELLs may confuse the word meanings of multiple-meaning words (e.g., *face*, *side*) or become frustrated when more than one math term is used in a sentence. (e.g., **Measure** the **height**, **width**, and **length** of the **object** below.) To help them overcome these obstacles, copy the following glossary pages for each student in your class. Consider adding the "Glossary: Math Verbs" on pp. 61–62 for additional vocabulary help. Your students will feel more comfortable with this challenging subject if they have a math resource to consult.

addend: any of the numbers that are added together (Example: In 9 + 4 = 13, both 9 and 4 are addends.)

addition: finding the sum, or total, by combining two or more numbers

analog clock: uses moving hour and minute hands to show the time

angle: the space between two straight lines or surfaces that touch or cross each other, measured in degrees

array: an arrangement of objects, pictures, or numbers in columns and rows

attribute: a characteristic that describes an object, such as size, shape, color, etc.

calendar: a chart that shows all the days, weeks, and months in a year

capacity: the amount that something can hold

cardinal number: a number used to show the amount of something; also called a counting number (Examples: 1, 2, 3)

Celsius (C): a measurement of temperature; water boils at 100°C and freezes at 0°C.

cent (¢): a unit of money used in the United States; 100 cents is equal to one dollar.

centimeter (cm): a measure of length in the metric system, equal to $\frac{1}{100}$ of a meter; 2.54 cm = 1 inch

chart: a drawing, graph, or table that shows information

circle: a flat, round shape

column: a vertical (up and down) group of objects; this is a column of numbers:

7

11

12

29

cone: a solid shape that has a circular base and one vertex (point where two or more straight lines meet)

corner: the place where two lines, edges, or sides of something meet

cube: a solid shape with six identical square faces

cylinder: a solid shape with two identical flat, circular ends (bases) and one curved side

day: a period of 24 hours, from midnight to midnight

decimal point: a dot used to separate a whole number and a fractional part of a whole number (Example: In 10.1, the dot separates the whole number 10 and the fractional number 1.)

difference: the result of subtracting one number from another; how much one number differs from another (Example: The difference between 7 and 2 is 5.)

digit: any one of the Arabic numerals, from zero to nine

digital clock: uses numbers, not hands, to show the time

dime: a United States coin worth ten cents

distance: the amount of space between two places; the length of a line between two points

dollar ($): the main unit of money in the United States; one dollar is equal to 4 quarters, 10 dimes, 20 nickels, or 100 pennies.

equal (to): the same as something else in size, value, or amount (Examples: $10.00 is equal to 10 one-dollar bills; 1 + 3 is equal to 4.)

equation: a statement in which one set of numbers or values is equal to another set of numbers or values; an equation always has an equals (=) sign.

even number: any number that can be divided exactly by 2; the last digit will be 0, 2, 4, 6, or 8.

expanded form/notation: writing a number so that the value of each digit is shown
(Example: 826 = 8 x 100 + 2 x 10 + 6 x 1)

face: any of the individual surfaces of a solid object (Example: A cube has six faces.)

Fahrenheit (F): a measurement of temperature; water boils at 212°F and freezes at 32°F.

foot (ft.): a measure of length that equals 12 inches

fourth (of): one of four equal parts of a whole (Example: Nadya ate $\frac{1}{4}$ of the pie, which means she ate one of four equal parts of the pie.)

fraction: a part of a whole number (Examples: $\frac{1}{2}$, $\frac{3}{4}$, $\frac{5}{8}$)

gallon (gal.): a measure of liquid that equals four quarts

graph: a diagram of values, usually shown as lines or bars

greater than (>): more than (Example: 9 > 8)

half (of): one of two equal parts of a whole (Example: Riley and Amir shared a pizza equally. They each ate half.)

half-circle/semicircle: half of a circle; one circle equals two semicircles.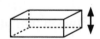

half hour: a unit of time equal to 30 minutes, or half an hour

height: the measurement of how high or tall something is

hexagon: a flat shape with six straight sides

horizontal: parallel to the ground; going side-to-side like the horizon

hour: a unit of time equal to 60 minutes

hundred(s): the whole number that is equal to 10 times 10, written as 100 (Example: There are three hundreds in 300.)

inch (in.): a measure of length that equals $\frac{1}{12}$ of a foot (Example: A standard paper clip is a little over one inch long.)

length: the measurement of how long something is; the distance from one end of something to the other end

less than (<): fewer than (Example: 8 < 9)

meter (m): a measure of length in the metric system; it is equal to 39.37 inches, or about 3 feet.

metric system: the system of weights and measures that is based on the meter and kilogram

mile (mi.): a measure of length that equals 5,280 feet

minute: a unit of time equal to 60 seconds

month: a period of between 28–31 days, or $\frac{1}{12}$ of a year

nickel: a United States coin worth five cents

number line: a line with numbers placed in their correct positions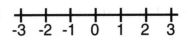

number sentence: an equation or inequality expressed using numbers and common symbols (Examples: 45 – 12 = 33; 26 > 21)

numeral: a symbol or name that stands for a number (Examples: 2, 29, fourteen)

object: something that you can see and touch but that is not alive

odd number: any number that cannot be divided exactly by 2; the last digit will be 1, 3, 5, 7, or 9.

ordinal number: a number that tells the position of something in a list (Examples: 1st, 2nd, 3rd)

ounce (oz.): a measure of weight equal to $\frac{1}{16}$ of a pound

parallelogram: a shape that has four straight sides; its opposite sides are parallel and equal in length, and its opposite angles are equal.

pattern: a repeating arrangement of shapes, colors, figures, or numbers

penny: the smallest unit of money in the United States; a coin worth one cent

pentagon: a flat shape with five straight sides

place value: the value of a digit in a number based on its position in the number; it is measured in tens, hundreds, thousands, etc. (Example: In 567, the place value of 5 is "hundreds.")

pound (lb.): a measure of weight equal to 16 ounces

prism: a solid shape with two identical ends (bases) and all flat sides (faces); the shape of the ends gives the prism its name. (Example: A triangular prism has two triangular ends [bases] and three flat sides [faces].)

process: the steps you take to achieve something

pyramid: a solid shape with a polygon as a base and triangular sides (faces) that meet at a point on top

quadrilateral: a plane (two-dimensional) shape with four straight sides and four angles (Examples: rectangle, rhombus, trapezoid)

quarter: a United States coin worth 25 cents

rectangle: a flat shape with four sides and four right angles

row: a horizontal (side to side) group of items; this is a row of numbers: 7   11   12   29

ruler: a long, flat piece of wood or metal used to measure and draw straight lines

scale: a machine used to weigh people or objects

second: a unit of time equal to $\frac{1}{60}$ of a minute

semicircle/half-circle: half of a circle; one circle equals two semicircles.

side: one of the lines that makes a flat shape (Example: A square has four sides.); one of the surfaces that makes a solid shape (Example: A cube has six sides.)

skip-counting: counting forward or backward by a number other than 1 (Example: Skip-counting by 2 is 2, 4, 6, 8, etc.)

sphere: a solid round shape; every point on the surface of the shape is the same distance from the center.

square: a flat shape with four equal sides and four right angles

standard form/notation: writing a number so that one digit is shown for each place value (Examples: 101, 963)

subtraction: taking one number away from another (Example: If you have 5 pens and you subtract 4, you will be left with 1 pen.)

sum: the result of adding two or more numbers (Example: The sum of 3 and 3 is 6, because 3 + 3 = 6.)

symbol: a design or an object that represents something else (Example: "+" is the symbol for "plus.")

symmetrical: having two parts that are exactly the same in shape, size, and arrangement

symmetry: a balanced arrangement of parts on either side of a line or around a central point

tally mark: a mark used to count and record information

temperature: how hot or cold something is, measured by a thermometer

ten(s): the whole number that is equal to 1 times 10, written as 10 (Example: There are three tens in 30.)

texture: how a surface or substance feels or appears

thermometer: an instrument used to measure temperature (how hot or cold something is)

third (of): one of three equal parts of a whole (Example: Kai ate $\frac{1}{3}$ of the apple, which means he ate one of three equal parts of the apple.)

thousand(s): the whole number that is equal to 10 times 100, written as 1,000 (Example: There are three thousands in 3,000.)

trapezoid: a shape that has four straight sides; only one pair of opposite sides is parallel.

triangle: a flat shape with three straight sides

unit: a single thing that is part of a larger group or whole

unit (measurement): an amount used as a standard of measurement (Example: Some units of time are second, minute, hour, and day.)

value: what something is worth

vertical: upright, or straight up and down

volume: the number of cubic units (cubes) that it takes to fill up an object

week: a period of seven days

weight: the measurement of how heavy something is

whole number: any positive number that does not have a fraction or decimal

width: the measurement of how wide something is; the distance from one side of something to the other

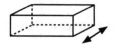

yard (yd.): a measure of length equal to three feet, or 36 inches

year: a period of about 365 days; the time it takes for Earth to make one complete trip around the sun

Math Language Connections *(cont.)*
Glossary: Math Verbs

In math, students are often asked to accomplish specific tasks. The verbs, or actions, used in directions may be unclear because the words are unknown or have multiple meanings. An understanding of what the directions ask will help students feel more comfortable with math in general. Consider photocopying these pages and attaching them to the "Glossary: Math Terms" (pp. 54–60) so that students have a complete glossary they can reference.

add (+): to combine two or more groups together (Example: Lindsey has $10.00. Phil has $5.00. How much do they have all together? They have $15.00 because $10.00 + $5.00 = $15.00.)

check: to look at something carefully

choose: to pick out something from a group (Example: You want to choose the correct answers when you take a test.)

circle: to draw a round line around something

compare: to show how two or more things are similar to or different from each other

count: to find the total number of things in a group; to say numbers in order, one by one

cross out: to draw a line or lines through something

decide: to make a choice or judgment about something

estimate: to make an informed guess about an amount, distance, or cost of something

evaluate: to look at something and think about its value

examine: to look at something carefully in order to learn more about it

explain: to make something clear so that it is easy for someone else to understand; to give a reason for something

figure out: to think about a problem until you find the answer; to understand or solve something

fill in: to add information (answers, numbers, etc.) to blank spaces

find: to discover, see, or get something

group: to arrange things by types

guess: to give an answer that may be right but you are not completely sure

label: to write a word or phrase that tells what someone or something is like *list:* to say or write things, one after the other

make: to do or create something (Example: Cynthia will make a bar graph.)

measure: to find a number that shows the size or amount of something

order: to put things into their correct place following some rule

predict: to say that something will or might happen in the future

record: to write down information or facts

save: to keep money to use in the future rather than spend it now

show: to tell someone how to do something by explaining it in words, writing, or with actions

solve: to find the correct answer to a problem or question

spend: to use money to pay for something

subtract (–): to take a number or amount from another number or amount (Example: Corinne had 5 oranges. She gave 2 to her friend. How many oranges does Corinne have left? Corinne has 3 oranges, because 5 – 2 = 3.)

tally: to count or record information; tally marks represent information.

Math Language Connections (cont.)
Confusing Language Patterns

One of the reasons ELLs struggle with math is that it contains confusing language patterns. Some of the most troublesome language patterns are listed below.

Language Pattern	Example	Remedy
Passive sentence structure	*Travis had 12 lemons. Eight lemons <u>were used</u> to make lemonade. How many lemons were left?*	Reword problem so it is active. *He used 8 lemons to make lemonade.*
Multiple-meaning words	*Make a <u>table</u> to show which coins Lena could have if she had 25¢.*	Reword the problem and discuss what it is asking. *Make a chart to show which coins Lena could have if she had 25¢.*
Comparisons	*Ari's plant is 4 inches tall. Ted's plant is 3 inches tall. Which plant is taller?*	Think aloud and/or use a diagram to illustrate the problem.
Connecting words that indicate relationships between parts of a sentence	*Jelan has 25¢, <u>but</u> she needs 55¢ to buy a pencil. How much more money does she need?*	Break sentences into parts. *Jelan has 25¢. She needs 55¢ to buy a pencil. How much more money does she need?*
Long, complex sentences (e.g., sentences with *if/then* construction)	*Jamal is reading a book that has 16 pages. <u>If</u> he read 5 pages on Monday and 4 pages on Tuesday, <u>then</u> how many pages does he have left to read?*	Simplify the language; break sentences into parts. *He read 5 pages on Monday. He read 4 pages on Tuesday. How many pages does he have left to read?*
Word choice	*Ella has 2 books, Juan has 3 books, and David has 1 book. How many books are there <u>in all?</u>*	Explain the phrase and then reword the question. *How many books do they have (all together)?*

Math Language Connections *(cont.)*
Cracking the Code: Word Problems

When teaching word problems, it's important to start at the beginning. Students need to develop language skills and become familiar with this type of problem. Building upon background knowledge helps to create a safe environment where students are willing to take risks and try again. The following tips will help make word problems comprehensible for your students.

Tips for Teaching Word Problems

- ✪ Use real-world examples. (e.g., Use the names of students in class for sample word problems.)

- ✪ Relate word problems to students' prior knowledge.

- ✪ Relate new concepts to topics of current study (e.g., learning to measure in centimeters during a science unit on growing plants).

- ✪ Pre-teach any unknown vocabulary in word problems.

- ✪ Match words to specific mathematical operations.

- ✪ Help students identify keywords.

- ✪ Help students understand how problems are phrased.

- ✪ Introduce and demonstrate academic words and phrases commonly used in word problems. Consider sharing the following examples:

• all	• each	• part(s)
• all together	• enough	• piece(s)
• also	• equally	• plus
• among	• group(s)	• remain
• between	• in all	• solve
• both	• increase	• some
• combine	• left	• sum
• decrease	• minus	• take away
• difference	• only	• total

- ✪ Provide students with reading comprehension strategies, such as the following, to help them understand word problems.

> - Read the problem twice.
> - Make inferences while reading.
> - Translate into your native languages, if necessary.

Fire Up Word Problems

Use the following recommendations to make word problems more accessible to your students—from simplifying the language to including illustrations. Then motivate your students to succeed using the tips below.

Help Students Succeed With Word Problems

★ Provide explicit directions and practice with word problems.

★ Provide daily hands-on practice that includes movements or experiments.

★ Use manipulatives and relevant props to engage students.

★ Ask students to create their own word problems.

Fire Up Word Problems *(cont.)*

Simplify language.

- ✪ Avoid connecting words, such as *and*, *but*, and *or*.

- ✪ Rephrase problems with shorter sentences and simplified vocabulary.

- ✪ Vary problems for student practice by changing numbers or labels.

- ✪ Use sentence frames (pg. 46) or templates for word problems. Change just the numbers or the topic. (e.g., In a problem asking "how many apples," change the wording to "how many pencils.")

Make connections with reading comprehension skills.

- ✪ Read word problems several times together as a class.

- ✪ Help students understand what the problem is asking. Think aloud and have students think aloud.

- ✪ Have students paraphrase what they read.

Show what is important.

- ✪ Help students identify necessary and unnecessary words and information.

- ✪ Have students cross out unnecessary, extra information.

- ✪ Demonstrate how to use the information in a problem to write a number sentence.

Model how to write word problems.

- ✪ Use people and things that students know something about so they can use their prior knowledge and the context to solve the problem.

- ✪ Have students practice writing and solving word problems in small groups (pg. 47).

- ✪ Create word problems that use the current vocabulary students are learning.

Include illustrations.

- ✪ Use drawings to help students understand word problems.

- ✪ Link the numbers to the pictures. (e.g., Use interactive whiteboard technology to allow students to physically match numbers with related pictures to illustrate what a word problem means.)

Cautions for Students

Discuss the following cautions for students to remember as they learn about word problems. Consider creating a poster or chart to display in class.

- ★ Word problems may have nothing to do with real life.
- ★ Some word problems have information you do not need.
- ★ Some word problems have extra words or numbers.
- ★ Some word problems have more than one correct answer.

Math Language Connections (cont.)
Cracking the Code: Word Problems (cont.)

Steps to Solving Word Problems

Discuss the following problem-solving steps to help your students think about how to solve word problems. Consider creating a poster or chart to display in class. Then review a word problem, such as the one below.

> 1. Read the problem.
> 2. Understand what it is asking.
> 3. Cross out unimportant information.
> 4. Decide what you will do to try to solve the problem.
> 5. Do the math.
> 6. Show your work.
> 7. Explain what you did orally and/or in writing.

Sample Word Problem

Using the steps above, discuss as a class how to solve the following sample problem. Focus more on steps 1–4; communicate about how to solve the problem rather than on finding the answer. Consider asking the questions below to model the problem-solving process.

> Ryan and Hannah picked 12 strawberries. Then they picked 36 blueberries. They picked 24 more blueberries than strawberries. They want to share the berries equally.
>
> 1. How many berries did they pick in all? *(12 + 36 = 48)*
> 2. How many berries will each person have? *(48 ÷ 2 = 24)*

✪ Which word(s) can we circle to help us understand what the problem is asking? *(share, equally)*

✪ What information is not needed to answer the problem? *(how many more blueberries than strawberries they picked)*

✪ What strategies can we use to think about the problem? *(addition, counting into piles)*

✪ What does it mean to divide? *(To "divide" means to count out evenly into two piles.)*

✪ How will we know if our answer makes sense? *(We can add the number of berries each person gets together to find out if it equals the total number of berries they picked.)*

Literacy instruction in math class helps students learn to read and write about math. Students need good reading comprehension skills for reading math texts, directions, and word problems. Consider incorporating the following reading and writing tips into your math curriculum.

Tips for Incorporating Reading and Writing Into Math Curriculum

- ✪ Consider ELLs' existing language skills and needs when planning lessons.

- ✪ If math word problems are too short to contain the context and language necessary for comprehension, rephrase the problems to help students understand.

- ✪ Use sentence frames (pg. 46) to teach the grammatical structures students will need to know to read directions and word problems.

- ✪ Incorporate word problems into reading comprehension activities.

- ✪ Explain that students cannot read a "story" problem in math the same way they would read a fiction story.

- ✪ Provide books about math topics and have students read and talk about their reading to become more familiar with math terms.

- ✪ Teach students how to write numbers correctly in English.

- ✪ Have students write out number sentences using words to become familiar with number words.

- ✪ Encourage students to write their own math problems.

- ✪ Use math journals to have students write about their math learning experiences.

- ✪ Have students refer to and use words to describe manipulative materials correctly.

Steps to Build Math Literacy

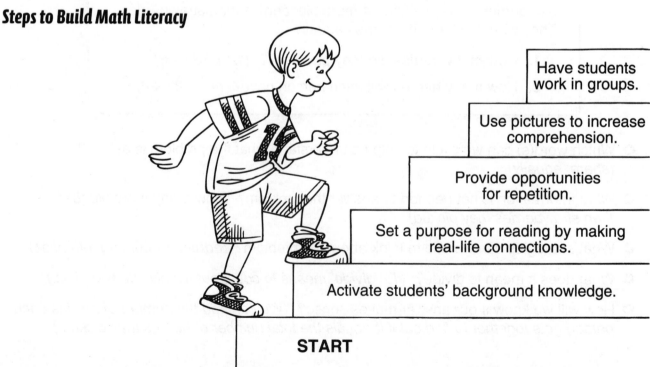

Have students work in groups.

Use pictures to increase comprehension.

Provide opportunities for repetition.

Set a purpose for reading by making real-life connections.

Activate students' background knowledge.

START

Math Language Connections (cont.)
Math Literacy (cont.)

Math Writing Activities

✪ Teach students signal words or prompt words that direct them to do certain processes in math. Use cards containing images, such as traffic-signal lights and arrows to display and teach students words to watch for and what they mean. Consider using the following words: *count, sort, compare, group, draw, list, solve, estimate, measure, explain*, and *show your work.*

✪ Read a book about math. (See pg. 110 for search suggestions.) Discuss the math concepts presented in the story. Talk about the story as a class, asking students for questions and math problems that could be included in the story. After a few experiences, have students write and illustrate their own math stories.

✪ Provide a table or chart to organize components of a word problem. Have students work in cooperative groups to complete the chart. Assign roles as desired. Teach students to check their work.

✪ Read a book together as a class and then make a "word cloud" using Wordle (pg. 109). Enter (copy/paste) a paragraph from the text. The program will help students see keywords and relationships between important concepts. Work together as a class to play with colors and other features of the program to see patterns. You may wish to enter text prior to the lesson and print out the word cloud for students. Distribute copies to students and have them find patterns and discuss the graphic. Students can then share their new understandings with the class. (*Note:* The Wordle shown here is made up of words and themes from this book.)

✪ Display and think aloud a math problem. Have students use blocks or draw boxes to help them understand math vocabulary, such as *older than, younger than*, and *half as many*. Consider sharing the following example:

It is three miles from Li's house to school. It is twice as far from Li's house to Pedro's. How far is it from Li's house to Pedro's?

| **Li's house** | | | | **school** |

| **Li's house** | | | | | | **Pedro's house** |

Possible thoughts: Twice as many means two times. Demonstrate that we need two times as many boxes to show the distance from Li's house to Pedro's. Point out that the problem only tells us the distance from Li's house to school. This is the starting measurement.

Practical Classroom Applications
Sample Lesson: What's It Worth?

Objective

Given demonstrations and experiences with money, students will learn about number-word and numeral values.

Vocabulary

cent (¢): a unit of money used in the United States; 100 cents is equal to one dollar.

compare: to show how two or more things are similar to or different from each other

count: to find the total number of things in a group; to say numbers in order, one by one

decimal point: a dot used to separate a whole number and a fractional part of a whole number

dime: a United States coin worth ten cents

dollar ($): the main unit of money in the United States; one dollar is equal to 4 quarters, 10 dimes, 20 nickels, or 100 pennies.

nickel: a United States coin worth five cents

penny: the smallest unit of money in the United States; a coin worth one cent

quarter: a United States coin worth 25 cents

Materials

- ✪ actual coins and dollar bills
- ✪ "Money Cutouts" (pg. 73), one set per pair of students
- ✪ envelopes, one per pair of students
- ✪ "Matt's Tea House" menu (pg. 74), one copy per pair of students and one copy for class display

Preparation

1. Photocopy and cut out the bills and coins from the money page. Put each set in an envelope. Make sure you have enough sets so that each pair of students has an envelope.

2. Photocopy the menu, one per pair of students. Prepare the menu for class display using an overhead projector or interactive whiteboard.

Opening

1. Display a variety of actual coins. Check students' existing background knowledge by asking questions such as these:
   - ★ What am I holding? (Students name a specific coin.)
   - ★ How much is it worth? (Students identify value.)
   - ★ Which is worth more, a dime or a quarter? (Students analyze the two number-word options and identify the greater value.)
   - ★ Which is worth more, 5¢ or 1¢? (Students analyze the two numeral options and identify the greater value.)

Practical Classroom Applications *(cont.)*
Sample Lesson: What's It Worth? *(cont.)*

Opening *(cont.)*

2. Display a variety of actual bills. Check students' existing background knowledge by asking questions such as these:

   ★ What am I holding? (Students name a specific bill.)

   ★ How much is it worth? (Students identify value.)

   ★ Which is worth more, a dollar or a quarter/dime/nickel/penny? (Students analyze the two number-word options and identify the greater value.)

   ★ Which is worth more, $5.00 or $10.00? (Students analyze the two numeral options and identify the greater value.)

Directions

1. Direct students' attention to the menu on display. Go over each item and dollar amount.

2. Divide students into pairs. Give each pair an envelope of the money cutouts and a copy of the menu.

3. Using the menu, give students different scenarios in which to use their money. Consider using the following scenarios:

   ★ Use your money ($15.25) to buy one item from each of the three categories: Tea, Small Bites, and Other Drinks. *(Sample answers: oolong tea, eggs and tomatoes, and a soft drink; black tea, dumplings, and juice)*

   ★ Use your money ($15.25) to buy three items. One must be a Tea to Go. *(Sample answers: black tea to go, white tea, and milk; white tea to go, soft drink, and juice)*

   ★ Buy enough items so that your total is exactly $13.00. *(Sample answers: green tea, spring rolls, and a soft drink; white tea, crispy tofu, and juice)*

   ★ Use your money ($15.25) to buy the greatest number of items. You may not buy more than one of each item. *(Sample answers: green tea, scallion pancakes, juice, soft drink, and milk; oolong tea, string beans, juice, soft drink, and milk)*

4. After each scenario, ask for volunteers to share their answers and then show their dollar amounts using their money. In the case of the last scenario, "Use your money to buy the greatest number of items," ask students to count their items and then raise their hands if they bought two items, then three items, then four items. Have pairs share their results for four items or more. Ask them to list the items they "bought" and then have them show what money they used to "pay" for the items. Compare the answers of several pairs.

Closing

Review money vocabulary, including *count* and *compare*, which were used during the activity. Discuss the meaning of decimal points in relation to money.

Extensions

1. Have each pair create their own menu. (If desired, have students add pictures.) Then have student pairs switch menus with other pairs. Students can use the same scenarios from the activity or create new ones.

2. Print out color pictures of the Small Bites menu items from the Internet. Label them and post them around the room. Have student pairs walk around the room with their menus and put numbers next to the appropriate menu items.

3. Bring in one or more dishes from the menu to share with the class. Doing so will expand their palates, as well as their appreciation for multicultural foods.

Interactive Whiteboard Option

Use the "drag and drop" feature to have students practice learning coin values and money vocabulary by matching with words.

ELL Tip

Consider having the menu translated into your ELLs' native languages.

Practical Classroom Applications (cont.)
Sample Lesson: What's It Worth? (cont.)

Money Cutouts

Matt's Tea House

Tea*
prices are by the pot

black $3.00

oolong $6.00

green $5.50

white $4.25

Small Bites
scallion pancakes (5) $5.25
   served warm, thin, and crispy

spring rolls (3) $6.00
   contains bamboo shoots, mushrooms, and cabbage

string beans $5.00
   fried with garlic and chilies

eggs and tomatoes $6.75
   scrambled with green onions

crispy tofu $7.50
   fried with salt and pepper

dumplings (6) $8.00
   contains shrimp or pork; available steamed or fried

Other Drinks
juice (apple or orange) $1.25

soft drinks $1.50

milk . . . . 95¢

*TEA TO GO: Each of our four types of tea comes in a 4 oz. package; prices are $9.98 (black tea), $12.19 (white tea), $15.75 (green tea), and $18.49 (oolong tea). Ask your server for more information.

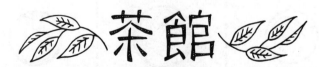

茶館

Practical Classroom Applications *(cont.)*
Sample Lesson: Think Like a Mathematician

Objective

Given a problem-solving demonstration, students will work independently and in small groups to think through the process of solving a sample math problem.

Vocabulary

mathematician: a person who is an expert (someone who specializes) in mathematics

pattern: a repeating arrangement of shapes, colors, figures, or numbers

process: the steps you take to achieve something

Materials

- ✪ chart paper for classroom display
- ✪ "The Future Mathematician" (pg. 78) (140 words, reading level 2.1), one copy for class display
- ✪ Sample Problems (pg. 78)
- ✪ beads, cards, other commonly counted objects, several for each pair of students (optional for extension activity)

Preparation

1. Display sentence frames on chart paper, a whiteboard, or an interactive whiteboard. Include the following questions:
   - ★ How many _____ are there?
   - ★ How many _____ do I need?

2. Prepare "The Future Mathematician" for class display on chart paper, an overhead projector, or an interactive whiteboard.

3. Photocopy and cut out the sample problems, making sure you have enough so that each student gets a problem. Color-code the problems by filling in each circle with a different color. Students will group themselves by color later in the lesson to work on their sample problems together.

Opening

1. Introduce the concept of a person who is a mathematician.

2. Read and discuss "The Future Mathematician." Ask the following questions:
   - ★ What real-life problems have you solved? Give an example.
   - ★ What things can you use to solve a problem?
   - ★ When have you made a model to help you find an answer to a problem?
   - ★ How can you use patterns to solve a problem?
   - ★ How can you use numbers to show your answer?
   - ★ How is your process the same as someone else's process?
   - ★ How is your process different from how someone else solves a problem?

Practical Classroom Applications (cont.)
Sample Lesson: Think Like a Mathematician (cont.)

Directions, Part I

1. Use diagrams to point out the structures of different types of math problems (e.g., addition or subtraction equations, measurement questions, word problems, telling time, counting money).

2. Think aloud to help students think through a process to solve a sample math problem, such as this:

> How can I divide the class into equal teams for PE? I can ask myself questions to set up a math problem. This will help me find the answer to my question.
>
> - How many students are in the class?
> - How many teams do I need?
> - How many students will be on each team?

3. Introduce sentence frames that students can use for reference as they think through the process of solving a math problem. Use the existing chart (from preparation), adding more examples. Consider sharing the following questions:

   ★ How can I act this out?
   ★ What objects can I use?
   ★ What picture can I draw?
   ★ What math symbols can I use?

4. Invite students to suggest additional sentence frames for class reference.

5. Give each student a color-coded problem. Have students work on their own problems for a few minutes, reading their sentences, drawing pictures, and completing sentence frames. Remind students to ask questions to think about how to solve the problems.

6. Have students find one or more classmates with the same colored circles. They will work in pairs or small groups to discuss how they solved their problems.

Directions, Part II

1. Restate the definition of a mathematician.

2. Review two ways mathematicians solve problems: (1) They ask questions, and (2) They use patterns to solve number problems.

3. Tell students to think like a mathematician, and then ask, "How can we use patterns to answer the question about dividing the class into equal teams for PE?"

4. Have students act out how to use patterns to find the answer. Give each student a colored tile or a number card. Have students arrange themselves in a color or number pattern.

5. Ask students what else they can do to find the answer. (e.g., They can group themselves by color or number.)

6. As time allows, discuss other sample math problems from the lesson. Ask students, "How can you use patterns to solve problems?"

Closing

1. Have students tell how they would solve a math problem, one step at a time.

2. Make reference cards of students' processes, with one step on each card.

Extensions

1. Give students the opportunity to practice using patterns to solve math problems.

2. Have students work with partners. Give pairs beads, cards, or other commonly counted objects and ask students to take turns counting their objects. Have students observe the different ways in which their partners count the objects (e.g., counting beads by 2s, counting cards by 5s, grouping like objects to count).

3. Pose additional math problems as time allows. Invite student pairs to share different ways they used patterns to count and solve problems.

Interactive Whiteboard Options

✪ Use the "drag and drop" feature to help students illustrate their processes for solving problems and to discuss sample math problems.

✪ Use the "hide and reveal" feature to help students visualize the questions.

ELL Tip

Work with a small group to discuss the sample problems. Draw sketches and give specific examples to help ELLs understand and discuss the story.

Practical Classroom Applications *(cont.)*
Sample Lesson: Think Like a Mathematician *(cont.)*

The Future Mathematician

Brian likes math. It is what he likes best in school. Brian wants to be a mathematician when he grows up.

Brian thinks about how to solve problems. He uses a process. He does the first step. Then he does the next step. Step by step, Brian solves the problem. He finds the answer.

His brother sees Brian work. He asks Brian how he solved the problem. Brian tells him. He draws pictures. Sometimes he puts in arrows and other symbols. Brian might write a number sentence to go with the picture.

Brian likes to play with numbers. He looks for patterns. He makes new patterns with his toys. Brian also likes to make models. Brian takes things apart. He puts them back together. He finds out how things work. This will help Brian use math when he gets older.

Sample Problems

○ I want to give each student a new pencil. Three students are absent. How many pencils do I need?

○ The class will go to the library. There are tables in the library. Five students will sit at each table. How many tables will we use?

○ Thirteen students in our class have turned in their permission slips for the field trip. How many students still need to turn in their permission slips?

○ There are 4 students in my reading group. We will each read 2 pages. How many pages will my whole group read?

○ I want to arrange the desks in groups for our science experiment this afternoon. There should be 4 desks in each group. How many groups will there be?

Practical Classroom Applications *(cont.)*
Sample Lesson: Math in Literature

Objective

Given a read-aloud experience, students will act out the story and then write math problems based on the characters and events in the story.

Vocabulary

save: to keep money to use in the future rather than spend it now

spend: to use money to pay for something

Materials

- ✪ *Alexander, Who Used to Be Rich Last Sunday*, by Judith Viorst (Scholastic, 1978)
- ✪ "Alexander Money Cutouts" (pg. 81), one set per student
- ✪ envelopes, one per student
- ✪ writing paper with space for illustrations
- ✪ crayons or colored pencils for each student
- ✪ classroom books containing math concepts

Preparation

1. Photocopy and cut out the dollars and coins from the money page. Make extra copies of the pennies, as there are only 16 pennies on the page and each set requires 31 pennies.

2. Put each set in an envelope. The set should include all of the dollars and coins listed in the story (3 x $1, 5 x 25¢, 6 x 10¢, 12 x 5¢, 31 x 1¢). Make sure you have enough sets so that each student has an envelope.

Opening

1. Ask students to share times when they have received money. If necessary, motivate students to share by asking questions such as the following:
   - ★ Have you ever found money on the ground? Where? When? How much was it?
   - ★ Has a relative ever given you money? Who was it? Why did he or she give it to you?

2. Invite students to discuss what they do when they have some money. Do they spend it or save it? What do they spend it on? For what items do they want to save their money?

Directions

1. Read *Alexander, Who Used to Be Rich Last Sunday.*

2. Discuss the math concepts presented in the story. Give each student an envelope. Have students act out the story, using the money cutouts to illustrate what happened to Alexander's money.

3. Work together as a class to talk through the story. Ask students questions to help them think of math problems that could be based on the story.

Practical Classroom Applications (cont.)
Sample Lesson: Math in Literature (cont.)

Directions (cont.)

4. Write sample math problems on the board. Consider sharing the following:
   - ★ Anthony has two dollars, three quarters, one dime, seven nickels, and eighteen pennies. How much money does Anthony have?
   - ★ Nicholas has one dollar, two quarters, five dimes, five nickels, and thirteen pennies. How much money does Nicholas have?
   - ★ Who has more money, Anthony or Nicholas? How much more money does he have?
   - ★ How much money does Alexander have after Grandpa and Grandma visit?
   - ★ On Sunday, how much more money does Anthony have than Alexander? (Remember, Alexander has one dollar from Grandpa and Grandma.)
   - ★ How much money did Alexander pay for each bet he made?
   - ★ After Nicholas won the bet, how much money did he have all together?

5. Have students write and illustrate their own math stories. Students may use the story as a model. Provide students with paper and crayons or colored pencils.

Closing

1. Invite volunteers to read their stories to the class.

2. As time allows, work as a class to write math problems based on students' stories for classmates to solve.

3. Ask students how the story they read relates to math concepts in real life. Have students share any personal experiences that relate to the lesson.

Extension
Invite students to explore math concepts in other favorite classroom books. After students read the stories, have them write math problems based on the characters and events in the story. This will help students see real-life connections in math.

Interactive Whiteboard Option
Students can "drag and drop" coin objects to demonstrate what happens to Alexander's money. Have them make up math problems using the amount of money Nicholas or Anthony has at the beginning of the story.

ELL Tip
Provide sentence frames for students when they write their own stories. Consider sharing the following:

- ★ Last Sunday, I had _____ dollar(s), _____ quarter(s), _____ dime(s), _____ nickel(s), and _____ pennies.
- ★ I went to the store and I bought _____.
- ★ I dropped a _____, and it fell down the drain in the street.
- ★ I went to a yard sale. I bought a _____ and a _____.
- ★ All I have left is _____ cents.

Alexander Money Cutouts

Practical Classroom Applications *(cont.)*
Sample Lesson: Exact Estimates

> **Objective**
> Given estimation experiences, students will estimate amounts, record data, and evaluate the accuracy of their estimates.

Vocabulary

check: to look at something carefully

guess: to give an answer that may be right but you are not completely sure

estimate: to make an informed guess about an amount, distance, or cost of something

evaluate: to look at something and think about its value

examine: to look at something carefully in order to learn more about it

record: to write down information or facts

Materials

- ✪ "Estimation Station Cards" (pg. 84), one set per student
- ✪ supplies for estimation stations: rulers, coins, a container, small items to be counted, a clear jar, a stopwatch
- ✪ "Estimate, Examine, Evaluate!" (pg. 85), one per student

Preparation

1. Photocopy the "Estimation Station Cards" and cut the cards apart. Make sure you have enough copies so that each student has one set of cards.

2. Set up a variety of "estimation stations" around the room. Each station should focus on a different math concept, such as the following:
   - ★ *distance*—Students will estimate the distance across a desk.
   - ★ *value of coins*—Students will estimate the value of coins in a container.
   - ★ *amount*—Students will estimate the number of items in a jar.
   - ★ *size*—Students will estimate the length and width of a math, science, or social studies textbook.
   - ★ *time*—Students will estimate how long it will take to write their full names.

Opening

1. Have students tell about a time when they guessed about something. Perhaps they guessed about how long it would take to get somewhere or about how many crackers to take out of a box so that each person could have the same amount.

2. Discuss the strategies they used to make their guesses as correct as possible.

Directions

1. Have two volunteers role-play a situation in which they estimate how much an apple weighs. Each person can guess the weight using standard or nonstandard units of measurement and write down an estimate. Have partners work together to check the actual weight by weighing and verifying the amount. Have students write down the actual weight. Together, the partners will decide which person's estimate was closer to the actual amount.

Directions *(cont.)*

2. Ask students to think about the processes the volunteers displayed in making estimates and finding the actual answer. What did the partners do first? What did they have to do to find the answer?

3. Distribute the "Estimation Station Cards," one set per student. Review the terms.

4. Have students arrange the cards in sequence to reflect the order in which they should complete the process of estimating and verifying an amount. Students should arrange their cards as follows: (1) Guess, (2) Estimate, (3) Check, (4) Record, and (5) Evaluate.

5. Divide students into five groups. Distribute copies of "Estimate, Examine, Evaluate!"

6. Have students visit the estimation stations set up around the room. Each group will have a turn at each station. Students should not measure the first time; they should observe and write down their estimates in the left column.

7. Next, have groups rotate through the stations again, this time measuring the items at the stations. (*Note:* Students will need to have someone in their groups monitor the stopwatch at the time station to determine how long it takes to write their full names.) Students will write the actual answers in the right column.

8. Have students evaluate the results by comparing their guesses with the actual amounts. Students should write a "+" or "–", depending upon if they guessed more than or less than the actual amount.

Closing

Discuss with the class the strategies they used to form their estimates, which strategies were most successful, and why.

Extension

Have students create their own estimation stations. Ask them to submit their ideas for approval before setting up their stations. Students may visit these stations when they have finished other classwork with time to spare. They should use additional copies of "Estimate, Examine, Evaluate!" to participate in their classmates' activities.

Interactive Whiteboard Options

✪ Display lines, shapes, or objects. Have students estimate the length or height and then measure with the interactive ruler.

✪ Display a random number/value of coins. Have students calculate a quick estimate when they first view the coins before they count to find the actual worth.

ELL Tip

Provide students with tips and tools for estimating. Have students use their fingers to estimate length and width of classroom objects, such as desks or books. Tell students to count by 2s or 5s to estimate the number of items in a jar.

Estimation Station Cards

Check

to look at something carefully

Estimate

to make an informed guess about an
amount, distance, or cost of something

Evaluate

to look at something and think
about its value

Guess

to give an answer that may be right
but you are not completely sure

Record

to write down information or facts

Practical Classroom Applications (cont.)
Sample Lesson: Exact Estimates (cont.)
Estimate, Examine, Evaluate!

Name: _____ Date: _____

Visit each estimation station. First, *estimate* (guess) each measurement. Write your guesses in the left column. Next, visit each station again to *examine* (check) the measurements. Write the correct answers in the right column. Last, *evaluate* your answers. Compare your guesses with the correct answers. If you guessed more than the actual amount, write a "+" sign in the small box. If you guessed less than the actual amount, write a "−" in the small box.

Distance	
I **think** my desk is about . . . length: _____ feet width: _____ feet	My desk is this big. length: _____ feet width: _____ feet

Value of coins	
I **think** the coins in the container are worth _____ .	The coins in the container are worth _____ .

Amount	
I **think** there are _____ items in the jar.	There are _____ items in the jar.

Size	
I **think** my textbook is about . . . length: _____ inches width: _____ inches	My textbook is this size. length: _____ inches width: _____ inches

Time	
I **think** it will take this long to write my full name. _____ minutes _____ seconds	It took this long to write my full name. _____ minutes _____ seconds

Practical Classroom Applications *(cont.)*
Sample Lesson: Explain Your Answer

> ### Objective
>
> Given a scenario, students will group and add multiple numbers and then explain their answers.

Vocabulary

explain: to make something clear so that it is easy for someone else to understand; to give a reason for something

value: what something is worth

Materials

- ✪ tokens, such as counting chips, tiles, laminated cards, or other counters; approximately 2 blue, 3 yellow, and 5 red per student
- ✪ star-shaped stickers
- ✪ blue, red, and yellow crayons or markers

Preparation

1. Randomly disperse and hide tokens of various colors around the room. Place two or three tokens with star stickers around the room.

2. Create a "story scene" appropriate for your class to describe what students will be doing as they gather the tokens. Relate it to student interests, a current holiday, or a topic of study (e.g., searching for buried treasure, finding objects in a virtual-reality world, digging for dinosaur bones or fossils, finding unusual insects).

3. Determine the point values you wish to assign to each color, based in part on your students' addition abilities (e.g., blue = 5 points, red = 3 points, yellow = 2 points).

Opening

1. Ask students to which color they would assign the highest point value, the next highest point value, and the third highest point value. Display sample tokens of blue, red, and yellow. Explain that often in the United States (and some other European countries) blue is used to indicate first place or being of high quality. In competitions in the United States, red may be awarded to second place and yellow to third place. Tell students that for this activity, point values will follow these colors, with blue having the highest point value, red the next, and yellow the lowest point value. Display one of each color token and its corresponding point value.

2. Teach students desired procedures and behaviors when gathering tokens and working in small groups.

Directions, Part I

1. Introduce the story scene. Explain that students will be finding and gathering tokens of various values. Assign groups.

Directions, Part I *(cont.)*

2. Have students move around the room and find tokens. You may wish to assign one group of students to each part of the room.

3. After the class has gathered the tokens, students will continue to work in small groups. While in groups, students will organize their tokens by color.

4. Give groups blue, red, and yellow crayons or markers. Have students make drawings of their organized tokens and simple number sentences to describe the total number of tokens they gathered.

Directions, Part II

1. Model for students how to use the values from their tokens to make number sentences. Write the values on the tokens for clarity.

2. Invite volunteers to demonstrate how to draw tokens with point values and write one or more descriptive number sentences. For example:

blue	blue	red	yellow	yellow
5	5	3	2	2

$$5 + 5 + 3 + 2 + 2 = 17$$
$$5 + 5 = 10$$
$$2 + 2 = 4$$
$$10 + 3 + 4 = 17$$

Directions, Part III

1. Explain that when students draw pictures with numbers that relate to their pictures, they are showing their work. The picture and numbers show how they made their number sentences. When people look at their pictures, numbers, and number sentences, they will see how the students got their answers.

2. Use an example to demonstrate that there may be more than one way to show how to arrive at the correct answer.

3. Ask students how it can help to show your work in picture form. Share the following answers, if needed:

   ★ If your answer does not match someone else's answer, you can look at the pictures and figure out which number sentences are correct.

   ★ If you have many objects, a picture can help you count how many objects you have all together if you group like objects.

Closing

1. Ask students to write *if/then* statements reflecting on how their number sentences and total token values would change if they had found a different number of tokens in each color.

Closing *(cont.)*

2. Invite those students who found the star tokens to share their *if/then* statements with the class using their tokens and writing number sentences on the board. Assign a value to the star tokens or allow students to do so.

Interactive Whiteboard Option

Select a background screen that relates to your sample story scenario. Place other objects (e.g., rocks, rivers, trees for a buried treasure scene) on the background and set the objects as the top layer. Use buttons to create tokens with corresponding colors and point values. "Drag and drop" tokens under the objects in the story scene to hide them. Set tokens as middle layer to place under objects on the top layer. Students can "drag and drop" tokens or use the magic eraser/marker function to reveal the treasure.

ELL Tips

1. Work with students in small groups to help them assign point values to colored tokens, group their tokens, and write number sentences.

2. Demonstrate how to change their models, drawings, and number sentences to form *if/then* statements.

Practical Classroom Applications *(cont.)*
Sample Lesson: *Show Your Digits*

Objective
Given digit cards, students will practice forming numerals and arranging digits to properly place commas in numbers.

Vocabulary

digit: any one of the Arabic numerals, from zero to nine

hundred(s): the whole number that is equal to 10 times 10, written as 100

numeral: a symbol or name that stands for a number

place value: the value of a digit in a number based on its position in the number; it is measured in tens, hundreds, thousands, etc.

thousand(s): the whole number that is equal to 10 times 100, written as 1,000

Materials

- ✪ "Digit Cards" (pg. 91), one set for each group of students
- ✪ cardstock
- ✪ envelopes, one per group of students

Preparation

1. Photocopy the "Digit Cards" onto cardstock. Laminate the cards, if desired.
2. Have adult volunteers assist in cutting out the cards for student use, or have students cut out the cards for fine motor skills practice.
3. Put each set of cards in an envelope.

Opening

1. Introduce new words as appropriate (e.g., *hundred, thousand*). Review place value as applicable.
2. Say new words and write sample numbers with commas on the board.
3. Have students work with partners to practice reading and writing number words in hundreds and thousands.

Directions

1. Pass out the envelopes containing the digits and comma.
2. Have students use their cards to create number patterns.
3. Invite volunteers (two to four students at a time, depending on students' understanding of place value) to arrange themselves in front of the room, holding digit cards.
4. Ask students to create two-, three-, and four-digit numbers. As a class, talk about what numbers the students are making.
5. Use the discussion to introduce the concept of using commas in American number notation.
6. Ask students where they would insert commas in the numbers demonstrated.

Practical Classroom Applications (cont.)
Sample Lesson: Show Your Digits (cont.)

Closing

Have students work in groups to create the greatest and least numbers possible with their digit cards, correctly placing the comma cards. Play a game in which group members (teams) take turns displaying their greatest/least numbers, saying them aloud, and correctly placing the commas. Those teams that successfully complete the given task may stay in the game for another round.

Interactive Whiteboard Option

Use the pen tool to have students practice writing numbers correctly with commas. Students may use different colors to designate place value.

ELL Tip

Provide word and number cards to help students say the words during the group closing activity.

Digit Cards

1	2	3
4	5	6
7	8	9
0	,	

Practical Classroom Applications (cont.)
Sample Lesson: All About Attributes

Objective

Given objects, students will discuss attributes, write sample math problems, and make inferences.

Vocabulary

attribute: a characteristic that describes an object, such as size, shape, color, etc.

estimate: to make an informed guess about an amount, distance, or cost of something

Materials

- ✪ "Different Attributes" chart (pg. 94)
- ✪ empty, plastic peanut-butter jars, one per group of students
- ✪ other common classroom containers, such as a pencil cup, book box, etc.
- ✪ beans

Preparation

Prepare the "Different Attributes" chart for class display on chart paper, an overhead projector, or an interactive whiteboard.

Opening

1. Use the "Different Attributes" chart to introduce the concept of attributes. Ask students to contribute their background knowledge and ideas to add to the chart.

2. Display several classroom containers and ask students to describe and compare the containers based on their attributes (size, shape, color, etc.).

3. Create a chart on the board to help students compare items.

Directions, Part I

1. Have students work in small groups to examine jars.

2. Have them discuss which attributes make the objects well suited for their purposes. Provide students with sample questions, such as the following:
   - ★ What are the attributes of these objects?
   - ★ How do we use these objects?
   - ★ How does each object's attribute fit its purpose (what we use it for)? (e.g., The size of a jar determines what can be put in it; if it is plastic, it doesn't break easily.)

3. Discuss with students other possible attributes an object can have. Consult the "Different Attributes" chart.

4. Ask groups to share their ideas for how jars can be used. List student ideas on the board or on chart paper for reference.

Practical Classroom Applications *(cont.)*
Sample Lesson: *All About Attributes* *(cont.)*

Directions, Part II

1. Have students work in their groups to write math problems about their jars. Encourage them to consider different purposes for the objects when writing problems. For example:

   * We store things in jars. About how many beans can we store in this empty plastic jar? How can I find out how many beans I can put in the jar without counting all of them? *(Fill the jar, and then estimate or guess.)* Once I have beans in the jar, how can I count them quickly to check my guess? *(Group beans by 10s; have each group member count a pile, and then add the totals together.)*

   * Some people drink water from jars. How much water can fit in this jar? Which size and shape of jar holds more water?

   * We could use a jar to roll out playdough.

   * You can grow sprouts from seeds in a jar.

2. Have students share their math problems with the class. Work one or two together as a class. If time allows, have students solve another group's problem.

Closing

1. Have students draw pictures of their jars, giving them different attributes. Motivate your students by asking them the following questions:

   * What would your jar look like if it were a different color?

   * What would your jar look like if it were smaller? If it were larger?

   * What would a square jar look like? Could you still use it for the same things, or would you have to store different things in it?

2. Have students share their drawings with partners and describe how they changed the attributes and ways to use the jars.

Extension

Have students group classroom objects by attributes. Challenge them to find one or more classroom objects that represent exceptions to a particular attribute. (e.g. When grouping long pencils, find a short one.) Students can then write math problems about their discoveries. (e.g., How much longer is Ivan's pencil than Kaylee's?)

Interactive Whiteboard Option

Have students use drawing options and features to design containers with a variety of attributes.

ELL Tip

Have students share with classmates the types of containers they use and the different ways they use them in their families/cultures.

Different Attributes

Attributes are characteristics that describe objects.

shape	rectangular, square, round
color	red, blue, orange
size	small, medium, large
height	short, tall
weight	light, heavy
density	thin, thick
texture	smooth, rough, bumpy

Examples of Objects with Attributes

- I have a blue, rectangular, medium-sized desk with a smooth top.

- My tangerine is orange and round with a thick and bumpy rind.

- The small tissue is thin and light.

Practical Classroom Applications *(cont.)*
Sample Lesson: Creating and Extending Patterns

Objective

Given verbal, visual, and physical cues, students will recognize and extend patterns.

Vocabulary

circle: to draw a round line around something; a flat, round shape

hexagon: a flat shape with six straight sides

parallelogram: a shape that has four straight sides; its opposite sides are parallel and equal in length, and its opposite angles are equal.

pattern: a repeating arrangement of shapes, colors, figures, or numbers

pentagon: a flat shape with five straight sides

rectangle: a flat shape with four sides and four right angles

square: a flat shape with four equal sides and four right angles

trapezoid: a shape that has four straight sides; only one pair of opposite sides is parallel.

triangle: a flat shape with three straight sides

Materials

- ✪ pattern blocks or basic geometric shapes, one set per pair of students
- ✪ "Geometric Shapes" (pg. 97), one for class display
- ✪ white cardstock or old file folders for pattern block cards
- ✪ colored pencils

Preparation

1. If a class set of pattern blocks is not available, use templates (or die cuts) to make paper geometric shapes.

2. Photocopy and enlarge "Geometric Shapes." Use the shapes that correspond to the class set of pattern blocks. Color the shapes, making each one a different color. Cut them out to make geometric shape cards.

Opening

1. Select several volunteers at a time to stand in front of the room. Hand each volunteer a geometric shape card in an order that creates a pattern. Ask the class what the cards show.

2. Discuss what makes it a pattern *(repeating, following a sequence)*. Introduce the words *repeat* and *sequence* as vocabulary words, if desired.

3. Read the shape words one at a time and have students repeat each word one or more times to assist with pronunciation.

4. Explain that patterns can be a repeated set of shapes or numbers, a shape or design that someone copies, or a set of actions. Tell students they will use patterns (a repeated set of actions) to learn to solve various types of math problems.

Practical Classroom Applications (cont.)
Sample Lesson: Creating and Extending Patterns (cont.)

Directions

1. Read a pattern orally for students to draw on their papers.

2. Display the geometric shape cards, if necessary, to provide visual cues. Students may copy the words, if desired.

3. Ask for volunteers to read patterns to provide further listening and speaking practice.

4. Pair up students, and have them create patterns using pattern blocks or geometric shapes.

5. One student in each pair should first create a pattern using the manipulative materials. His or her partner will read the pattern back.

6. Have students switch roles so each partner practices creating a pattern, identifying geometric shapes, speaking, and listening.

7. To follow up, have students individually create patterns and draw their patterns on paper. Students should label their patterns with the appropriate geometric words. If desired, provide labels for beginning ELLs or younger students to cut and glue.

Closing

Have students share or display their patterns for the class. Invite students to explain whether their patterns are repeating or sequential patterns and how they know.

Extensions

1. Invite students to work with their partners or other pairs of students in groups of four to extend patterns.

2. Have students give examples of how patterns are used in their homes or cultures.

Interactive Whiteboard Option

Have students use shape, duplicate, and group features to create sets or patterns of shapes.

ELL Tips

1. Model how to explain if a pattern is repeating or sequential and how you know.

2. Have ELLs share with partners during the closing activity. ELLs can practice explaining the pattern types and listing the shapes before volunteering to share with the class.

Practical Classroom Applications (cont.)
Sample Lesson: Creating and Extending Patterns (cont.)

Geometric Shapes

circle

square

triangle

rectangle

pentagon

hexagon

trapezoid

parallelogram

Practical Classroom Applications (cont.)
Sample Lesson: Place Value

Objective

Given demonstrations and examples, students will manipulate number cards and write numbers to express an understanding of place value.

Vocabulary

digit: any one of the Arabic numerals, from zero to nine

hundred(s): the whole number that is equal to 10 times 10, written as 100

place value: the value of a digit in a number based on its position in the number; it is measured in tens, hundreds, thousands, etc.

ten(s): the whole number that is equal to 1 times 10, written as 10

Materials

- ✪ straws, enough to bundle a few groups of ten
- ✪ rubber bands
- ✪ whiteboard, overhead transparency, or chart paper and appropriate markers in multiple colors
- ✪ cardstock or index cards, at least two per student
- ✪ "Digit Cards" (from "Show Your Digits" sample lesson, pg. 91), one set for each group of students (optional for extension activity)
- ✪ white paper, $8 \frac{1}{2}$" x 22" (or tape/glue two pieces of plain paper together), one strip per pair of students (optional for extension activity)

Preparation

1. Prepare a class set of number cards by writing one digit on each card. If desired, write digits in different colors to correspond to the colors you will use in step two of the directions.

2. Prepare strips of paper, if necessary, for extension activity.

3. Prepare "Tens" and "Ones" signs for use in step five of the directions, if desired.

Opening

1. Show students groups of straws banded together in groups of ten.

2. Invite a volunteer to draw a picture of the physical object(s). Ask students what the straws represent.

3. Ask students how they can use numbers to represent the objects and pictures.

4. Tell students that some number systems use markers to show the value of ones, tens, and hundreds. We group single items to form groups of ten (and groups of ten to form a group of one hundred). Then we use the order of digits in a number to show how many of each group (ones, tens, and hundreds) is present.

   Optional note: Depending on your students' prior knowledge and abilities, you may wish to have them share numbering systems in their cultures to compare with our system of place value.

Directions

1. Display the group(s) of straws again.

2. Write the number on the board, using different colors to represent the ones place and the tens place. Explain that we know the value of a digit by its place in the number.

3. Explain that as we write down what we say, the number of tens goes on the left, and the amount less than ten goes on the right.

   ★ Demonstrate by saying "twenty-six," and writing "26." To support visual learners, show two groups of straws and six individual straws.

   ★ Tell students to remember that the larger amount (the tens place) is first (to the left of the ones place). For example, we say the largest value first with money. (e.g., I have 4 dimes and 2 pennies, which is 42¢.)

4. Have students practice place value with number cards. Pair each student with a partner. Each student should have two or more number cards.

5. Review with students the order in which they should stand so that the person calling the number will read his or her number correctly. For additional help, place "Tens" and "Ones" markers on the floor to help students remember where to stand.

6. Call out a number and have pairs of students stand in the correct order to display the number.

7. Have volunteers take turns calling out a number. This allows students to hear different voices speaking numbers in English. Partners will arrange themselves to display the number as before.

8. If students know number words, write a number on the board and have them write the correct words to signify the place value of the digits. For example, write the number "35" on the board. Students will write "thirty-five."

Closing

1. Have students discuss with partners how they can remember the correct place value of digits in a number.

2. Call on volunteers to share with the class how to read and identify the place value of digits in a number.

Extensions

1. Pair up students. Give each pair a set of "Digit Cards" and a strip of paper. Have students make a number line, numbered by tens (for a two-digit activity).

2. Call out a number. Have students use their digit cards to place the number over the zero in the ones place on the appropriate part of the number line.

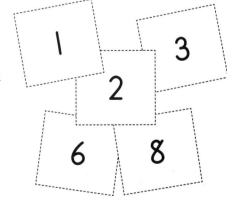

Practical Classroom Applications *(cont.)*
Sample Lesson: Place Value *(cont.)*

Extensions *(cont.)*

3. Challenge students to quiz each other by placing numbers on the number line to practice their understanding of place value.

Interactive Whiteboard Option

Use different sounds to represent digits in the ones, tens, and hundreds places to help students remember place value.

ELL Tip

When calling out a number for the extension activity, hold up a card for students to see the number at the same time they hear the number.

Practical Classroom Applications *(cont.)*
Sample Lesson: Measurement

Objective

Given pictures and objects, students will investigate and measure to gain a greater understanding of nonstandard and standard U.S. (customary) measurements.

Vocabulary

capacity: the amount that something can hold

distance: the amount of space between two places; the length of a line between two points

foot (ft.): a measure of length that equals 12 inches

gallon (gal.): a measure of liquid that equals four quarts

height: the measurement of how high or tall something is

inch (in.): a measure of length that equals $\frac{1}{12}$ of a foot

length: the measurement of how long something is; the distance from one end of something to the other end

measure: to find a number that shows the size or amount of something

metric system: the system of weights and measures that is based on the meter and kilogram

mile (mi.): a measure of length that equals 5,280 feet

ounce (oz.): a measure of weight equal to $\frac{1}{16}$ of a pound

pound (lb.): a measure of weight equal to 16 ounces

ruler: a long, flat piece of wood or metal used to measure and draw straight lines

volume: the number of cubic units (cubes) that it takes to fill up an object

weight: the measurement of how heavy something is

width: the measurement of how wide something is; the distance from one side of something to the other

yard (yd.): a measure of length equal to three feet, or 36 inches

Materials

- ✪ "Ways We Measure" (pg. 104), one copy for class display
- ✪ "My Measurements" (pg. 105), one copy per student
- ✪ rulers and yardsticks
- ✪ pictures or objects to illustrate weight (e.g., canned goods, nuts, fruit, coins)
- ✪ pictures or objects that represent volume (e.g., milk jugs, a picture of a barrel, a few kernels of wheat, a bottle of food coloring)

Preparation

Prepare the "Ways We Measure" chart for class display on chart paper, an overhead projector, or an interactive whiteboard.

Note: Many ELLs may have learned the metric system. Begin with basic units of measurement, such as inches, feet, pounds, cups, etc., to teach students our measurement system.

Practical Classroom Applications *(cont.)*
Sample Lesson: Measurement *(cont.)*

Opening

1. Divide students into groups. Assign each group a topic related to measurement, such as distance, capacity, or weight. More than one group may have the same topic. Have students discuss their topics for a few minutes.

2. Project the "Ways We Measure." Ask students what they know about each form of measurement, and write keywords or phrases next to the related images.

3. Show students a world map. Ask a volunteer to locate Europe on the map.

4. Explain that the U.S., or "customary," measurement system was developed in Europe over a long period of time, and settlers brought it with them to the United States. Remind students that many other countries now use the "metric" system, which was developed at a later time.

Directions, Part I

1. Introduce the concept of linear measurement, or measuring the length, distance, or height of something. Explain that people long ago measured distance by using items they had on hand.

2. Ask students to compare their hands or feet with classmates'. Ask, "Are they the same?" Explain that since people used what was available to measure; that is, parts of their bodies, not every measurement was exactly the same. We would say that their measurements are nonstandard (not all exactly alike) or estimates (close guesses).

3. Teach units of measurement as follows:

   * distance from the tip of the nose to the fingertip = a yard

   * distance from the first (closest to nail) knuckle to the second knuckle (or the width of a thumb) = an inch

   * size of a man's foot = a "natural" foot (9.8 inches) (Our 12" foot came from Rome.)

   * length of 1,000 paces of a Roman legion = mile (Our measurement for "mile" also came from Rome. A pace was two steps, right and left foot, about five feet. A mile, then, was about 5,000 feet.)

4. Ask the class, "Which measurement do we commonly use to measure the height of people?"

5. Ask volunteers to demonstrate each unit of measurement described.

6. Distribute copies of "My Measurements." Have students practice measuring items in the classroom using their hands and feet. Students may need to work in pairs to help each other hold objects. If students are familiar with using common measuring tools, such as rulers, have them check their work.

Directions, Part II

1. Use a picture to introduce and teach measurements for weight. Tell the class that merchants in England said a pound had 16 ounces, which can be easily divided into halves, fourths, and eighths. This is the pound we use today for most things.

Practical Classroom Applications *(cont.)*
Sample Lesson: Measurement *(cont.)*

Directions, Part II *(cont.)*

2. Have students practice weighing common objects in the classroom to find things that weigh one ounce and one pound. Have students take notes on their "My Measurements" pages.

3. Have students draw pictures of objects that weigh one ounce or one pound to create mental images of these common weight measurements.

Directions, Part III

1. Tell students that we measure volume, or amount of liquid, in gallons, with smaller increments in fluid ounces. Display an actual milk jug or a picture of one. Invite students to imagine the jug full of wheat kernels. Tell the class that one of the early gallon measurements was equal to 8 pounds of wheat. A gallon as measured today is exactly 231 cubic inches.

2. Explain that some liquids were measured in barrels, although exact amounts varied. Summarize with the statement that we use two units for measuring volume, U.S. liquid and U.S. dry.

Closing

Have students write one or more sentences similar to the following sentence frames:

* ★ A _____ will help me remember how long an inch is. (e.g., My thumb will help me remember how long an inch is. I can use the distance between the first and second knuckles on my thumb to measure about an inch.)

* ★ I know that a(n) _____ weighs about one pound. (e.g., I know that a box of crackers weighs about one pound.)

* ★ I have one cup of _____ to drink at lunch. (e.g., I have one cup of milk to drink at lunch.)

Extensions

1. Invite students to illustrate their sentences.

2. Compile student pages into a class book to help students remember and learn standard units of measurement.

Interactive Whiteboard Option

Use a ruler graphic and pen colors to help students learn how to read a ruler.

ELL Tip

Have students work with native English speakers to complete the "My Measurements" page.

Ways We Measure

Distance

_____

_____

_____

_____

_____

Capacity

_____

_____

_____

_____

_____

Weight

_____

_____

_____

_____

_____

My Measurements

Object	My Measurement	Actual Measurement
unsharpened pencil	8 knuckle lengths	7 $\frac{1}{2}$ inches

Practical Classroom Applications (cont.)
Assessments

Teachers assess student work to determine how well students have learned new math concepts. In math it is particularly important for students to understand one concept before moving on to the next, since math tends to build upon a foundation. Students can demonstrate their learning in a variety of ways: by completing in-class and homework assignments, by performing a process or series of actions to demonstrate understanding, or by taking a test.

When planning assessments, be aware of your students' . . .

- language proficiency levels.
- cultural backgrounds.
- educational backgrounds.
- learning styles.
- individual goals and needs.
- progress and growth over time.

Prepare for assessments using the following tips:

- ✪ Conduct a pre-assessment to determine areas in which ELLs will need extra support and instruction.

- ✪ Design assessments that focus on the concepts you want students to learn.

- ✪ Before selecting an assessment technique, consider the learning goals. Then decide which approach would be most appropriate—informal (formative) or formal (summative).

- ✪ Match the language of instruction to the language of assessment.

Use a variety of procedures and techniques to assess students, such as the following:

- ✪ Formative assessments (e.g., class discussions, observations, comprehension checks, student portfolios, math journals)—to make adjustments in teaching, to help students identify changes they need to make in their learning, to monitor student progress across all math standards

- ✪ Summative assessments (e.g., quizzes or tests after a unit of study)—to check comprehension of material studied and realize what requires reviewing

- ✪ Student portfolios—to demonstrate student growth and learning in math; include formative and summative assessments

- ✪ Rubrics—to assess student math assignments or math journals

Connect homework to assessments using the following tips:

- ✪ Share learning goals with students.

- ✪ Use predictable formats for homework assignments and assessments.

- ✪ Provide visuals to help students understand math homework.

Practical Classroom Applications *(cont.)*
Assessments *(cont.)*

Connect homework to assessments using the following tips:

- ✪ Check the language of homework problems to make sure it is simple and clear for ELLs to understand.

- ✪ As a class, review examples of student work that meet assessment or rubric guidelines so students can see effective problem-solving solutions.

Teach students to evaluate themselves using the following tips:

- ✪ Involve students in informal assessments. Have students create simple card games to use with peers to review math facts.

- ✪ Consider using translation resources to translate a simple rubric so students can first learn the concept of self-assessment in their primary languages.

- ✪ Teach students how to use rubrics to evaluate their work.

Modify assessments using the following tips:

- ✪ Differentiate assessments based on students' English proficiency and classroom experiences.

- ✪ Modify test language to reduce the amount of complex language structures; this helps all students.

- ✪ Check questions on assessments for readability. Do the questions contain all the words necessary for a sentence to grammatically make sense?

- ✪ Simplify questions, if possible.

- ✪ Read questions orally as students follow along.

- ✪ Allow extra time for students to complete assessments.

- ✪ Provide word-to-word dictionaries (that do not include definitions).

Teacher Resources
Websites for Educators

Center for Applied Linguistics (CAL): *http://www.cal.org*

CAL publishes research, teacher education, instructional materials, etc., about language, literacy, math language and literacy, assessment, and culture. For a complete list of their math ELL resources, go to "Search" at the top, right-hand side of the page and type "math."

Center on Instruction (COI): *http://www.centeroninstruction.org*

Center on Instruction is funded by the U.S. Department of Education and is one of five national content centers. The center focuses on seven topics, one being English language learners. Within that topic, there are more than 40 resources—varying from instructional models and strategies to professional development modules. Content is free and easy to access.

Classroom Zoom: *http://www.classroomzoom.com*

Classroom Zoom is an online subscription service created by Teacher Created Resources. Subscribers to the service have access to more than 11,000 printable lessons—all searchable by grade and subject. Members can also create custom math worksheets. Additionally, there are more than 1,000 free lessons available to nonmembers.

Dave's ESL Café: *http://www.eslcafe.com*

This site is maintained by its founder, Dave Sperling—a teacher with both ESL and EFL instructional experience. Since 1995, Dave has devoted much time and energy to creating a site dedicated to providing ideas for ESL teachers, as well as support for ELLs. On this site, you can find teacher forums, lesson ideas, and even job boards. For math activities, go to "STUFF FOR TEACHERS," then select "Idea Cookbook," and finally "Math."

Everything ESL.net: *http://www.everythingesl.net*

Judie Haynes, an ESL teacher from New Jersey with more than 32 years of experience, is the main contributor to this site, which includes lesson plans, teaching tips, and various resources for ESL teachers. There is also a question-and-answer section where visitors are encouraged to ask questions (to Judie) and give responses. For math materials, go to "Search with Google™" and type "math."

Harcourt School Publishers: *http://www.hbschool.com/glossary/math2/index.html*

This site offers a K–6 multimedia math glossary. The student-friendly definitions include colorful, visual examples.

Math Is Fun!: *http://www.mathsisfun.com*

Since 2000, this site has been helping teachers and students with math education. It offers math worksheets, activities, games, and an extensive illustrated math dictionary. The site also covers each branch of math, including numbers, algebra, geometry, data, and measurement.

Math Playground: *http://www.mathplayground.com*

Since 2002, this site has been regularly updated by Colleen King—a learning center mathematics teacher. Her goal has always been to create fun ways for students to practice math. The site contains a variety of activities, including logic games, math videos, and word problem practice.

Math TV: *http://www.mathtv.com*

This membership site offers video explanations for basic math (numbers), algebra, geometry, trigonometry, and calculus problems. Many of the videos include Spanish versions. For each skill, there are a number of sample problems to choose from.

National Center for Education Evaluation and Regional Assistance (NCEE): *http://www.ies.ed.gov/ncee*

The National Center for Education Evaluation and Regional Assistance (NCEE) is one of four centers of the Institute of Education Sciences (IES). Its mission is to provide evidence for education practice and policy and then share the information broadly. Through this site, you can access reports and studies relevant to English language learners (among many other topics).

National Clearinghouse for English Language Acquisition and Language Instruction Educational Programs (NCELA): *http://www.ncela.gwu.edu*

This site contains information and resources dedicated to Title III (organized by state), standards and assessments, and grants and funding. It also offers webinars, publications (including NCELA's *AccELLerate*), and a resource library to aid ESL teachers in the classroom. Search for math articles and resources using the search bar in the upper, right-hand corner of the main page.

Reading Rockets: *http://www.readingrockets.org*

Reading Rockets, a project created by WETA, is aimed to inform educators and parents on how to teach children to read, why some children struggle with reading, and how adults can help struggling children. The project includes PBS television programs; online resources, such as podcasts and blogs; and professional development opportunities. Strategies, reading guides, and newsletters can also be found on the site. For articles specific to math, type "math" in the search box at the top, right-hand side of the page.

Teachers First: *http://www.teachersfirst.com*

Helping educators since 1998, Teachers First offers teachers more than 12,000 classroom and professional resources, including rubrics, lesson plans, and tips for working with parents, substitutes, and technology. For math-specific classroom resources, go to "Classroom Resources," select the intended grade level(s), and search "math."

TrackStar: *http://trackstar.4teachers.org*

TrackStar helps you create and store online lessons and activities. These interactive lessons are called Tracks. To make a Track, you simply add annotations and website addresses. Or you can access the hundreds of thousands that have been made by other educators. To find math ELL tracks, click on "Browse by Subject/Grades" under "Find a Track." Next, in the Subject(s) section, select "English as a Second Language" and "Math."

Wordle: *http://www.wordle.net*

Wordle is a free resource that generates "word clouds" from text that you provide. The more often a word appears in a text, the larger the word appears in a cloud. Clouds can be modified with different fonts, layouts, and color schemes. Once made, the clouds can be saved (or not), printed out, and posted on anything—from cards to T-shirts!

Teacher Resources (cont.)
Translation Websites

Bing Translator: *http://www.microsofttranslator.com*

This free translator can translate over 30 languages. Users have the option of copying and pasting text into a box or entering website addresses (for full website translations). Additionally, the site offers Tbot—an automated "buddy" that provides translations for Windows Live Messenger. Using the Tbot translator, friends who speak other languages can have one-on-one conversations. Users simply need to add *mtbot@hotmail.com* to their Messenger contacts.

Dictonary.com Translator: *http://translate.reference.com*

This free translator can translate over 50 languages and up to 140 characters at a time. The site also offers a separate Spanish dictionary and translator. At the top of the page, select "Spanish" to view the translator box, as well as the Spanish word of the day, phrase of the day, and grammar tip of the day. The site contains over 750,000 English-Spanish dictionary definitions, example sentences, synonyms, and audio pronunciations.

Google Translate: *http://translate.google.com*

This free translator can translate over 60 languages. Users have the option of copying and pasting text into a box, uploading entire documents, or entering website addresses (for full website translations).

SDL FreeTranslation.com: *http://www.freetranslation.com*

This free translator can translate over 30 languages. Users have the option of copying and pasting text into a box or entering website addresses (for full website translations). The site also offers spoken or emailed translations. A free iPhone application and Facebook translator can also be downloaded.

Tips for Online Searches

- ✪ Add "ELL" and "math" to any search term to narrow the focus.

- ✪ Search for any strategy, for example "ELL math journals" or "ELL math mnemonics."

- ✪ Search for math literature using phrases, such as "read about math," "math books for 2nd graders," or "math in literature."

- ✪ Look up the following keywords or phrases:

  - ★ teaching strategies
  - ★ sentence frames
  - ★ literacy
  - ★ assessment
  - ★ graphic organizers
  - ★ rubics

Note: Consider locating specific articles and then cutting and pasting the information into text for student use, as some advertisements may be inappropriate for students.

Bibliography

Bassoff, Tobey. "Breaking the Language Barrier in Mathematics." Teachers Network. Accessed February 20, 2012. http://www.teachersnetwork.org/ntol/howto/eslclass/mathematics.htm.

Bresser, Rusty, and Kathy Melanese. "Supporting English Language Learners in Math in Regular or Mainstream Classrooms." Webinar. Accessed February 20, 2012. http://www.mathsolutions.com/webinars/ell/MathSolutionsWebinar_ELL_1209.pdf.

Burns, Marilyn. "How to Make the Most of Math Manipulatives." *Instructor*. Accessed February 20, 2012. http://teacher.scholastic.com/lessonrepro/lessonplans/instructor/burns.htm.

Dalton, Bridget, and Dana L. Grisham. "eVoc Strategies: 10 Ways to Use Technology to Build Vocabulary." *The Reading Teacher* 64, no. 5 (February 2011): 306–17.

Irujo, Suzanne. "So Just What Is the Academic Language of Mathematics?" *The ELL Outlook*, May/June 2007. Accessed February 20, 2012. http://www.coursecrafters.com/ELL-Outlook/2007/may_jun/ELLOutlookITIArticle1.htm.

——. "Teaching Math to English Language Learners: Can Research Help?" *The ELL Outlook*, March/April 2007. Accessed February 20, 2012. http://www.coursecrafters.com/ELL-Outlook/2007/mar_apr/ELLOutlookITIArticle1.htm.

Janzen, Heidi. "Helping English Language Learners in the Math Classroom." Teaching Today. Accessed February 20, 2012. http://www.glencoe.com/sec/teachingtoday/subject/help_ELL_math.phtml.

Little, Mary, and Shelby Robertson. "Increasing Educators' Implementation of the Concrete-to-Representational-to-Abstract (CRA) Model in K–12 Classrooms." Lecture, Teacher Education Division, Texas, Dallas, November 08, 2008. Accessed February 20, 2012. http://docs.google.com/viewer?a=v&q=cache:XJ06vNIrbuEJ:rtitlc.ucf.edu/documents/Pres/TED_11_08_08.pdf what do students need to achieve math learning K2FCHiyGwX5IezEeoUde60OZvXmQcoJJqQ5rnvFd MuIoqoLReBY7ASwctCG_4sPxR45id47cQP0AD4nRToUc6bMgHUaZfEvSCL5dxjkO68emtJvR K&sig=AHIEtbTdzbfyDlGDaTUt8_8FLQ1x0M-LwQ.

"Math Study Skills: Learning Styles." Mission College. February 06, 2007. Accessed February 20, 2012. http://salsa.missioncollege.org/mss/stories/storyReader$38.

"Mathematics Learning—Word Problem Solving." State University.com. Accessed February 02, 2012. http://education.stateuniversity.com/pages/2206/Mathematics-Learning-WORD-PROBLEM-SOLVING.html.

New Jersey Mathematics Coalition. "Standard 10: Estimation." New Jersey Mathematics Curriculum Framework. 1996. Accessed February 20, 2012. http://dimacs.rutgers.edu/nj_math_coalition/framework/ch10/ch10_k-02.html.

New Teacher Center. "Six Key Strategies for Teachers of English-Language Learners." Alliance for Excellent Education. December 2005. Accessed February 20, 2012. http://www.all4ed.org/files/archive/publications/SixKeyStrategies.pdf.

Bibliography *(cont.)*

Scholastic Children's Dictionary. New York: Scholastic Reference, 2002.

TESOL. *TESOL ESL Standards for Pre-K–12 Students.* Alexandria, Virginia: TESOL, 1997.

Tewksbury, Barbara J., and R. H. Macdonald. "Part 2.2: Teaching Strategies." Carleton College: On the Cutting Edge. 2005. Accessed February 20, 2012. http://serc.carleton.edu/NAGTWorkshops/coursedesign/tutorial/strategies.html.

"Using Mnemonic Instruction to Teach Math." The Access Center. Accessed February 20, 2012. http://www.k8accesscenter.org/training_resources/mnemonics_math.asp.

Wetzel, David R. "Teaching Strategies in Math for ESL Students: Instructional Techniques That Increase Comprehension of Concepts." Suite 101. September 23, 2009. Accessed January 3, 2012. http://www.suite101.com/content/teaching-strategies-in-math-for-esl-students-a152018.

Williams, Margaret M. "Adapting Math Story Problems for ESL Students: Making Word Problems Comprehensible for English Language Learners." Language Study @ Suite 101. August 17, 2009. Accessed February 20, 2012. http://www.suite101.com/content/adapting-math-story-problems-for-esl-students-a139737.

———. "Strategies to Support ESL Students in Math: Scaffolding Tips for ELL Math Instruction." Language Study @ Suite 101. May 10, 2009. Accessed February 20, 2012. http://www.suite101.com/content/strategies-to-support-esl-students-in-math-a116386.

Winsor, Matthew S. "Bridging the Language Barrier in Mathematics." *Mathematics Teacher* 101, no. 5 (December/January 2007/2008): 372-78. Accessed February 20, 2012. http://www.tsusmell.org/downloads/Products/Articles/MELL_Winsor_MT_Article.pdf.